Library of
Davidson College

# Distressed Workers
# in the Eighties

**by Daniel H. Saks**
Professor of Education Policy and Economics,
Vanderbilt University;
and Associated Staff Member,
Economic Studies Program,
Brookings Institution

 **Committee on New American Realities**

331.09
S158d

**Distressed Workers in the Eighties**

NAR Report #1
NPA Report #202

Price: $7.00

ISBN 0-89068-070-1
Library of Congress
Catalog Card Number 83-63104

Copyright 1983
by the National Planning Association
A voluntary association incorporated under the laws
of the District of Columbia
1606 New Hampshire Avenue, N.W.
Washington, D.C. 20009

  84-219

# Contents

**Distressed Workers in the Eighties**
by Daniel H. Saks

Committee on
New American Realities / inside front cover

A Statement by the Committee / vi
    Members of the Committee Signing the Statement / ix

Acknowledgments / x

*Chapter 1*
**Introduction / 1**
    Definition of Distress in the Labor Market / 1
    Classifying Causes and Solutions of Distress / 5

*Chapter 2*
**The Labor Market in the 1980s / 7**
    The Macroeconomic Environment / 7
    The Supply Side / 8
    The Demand Side / 12
    Conclusion / 16

*Chapter 3*
**Youth in Labor Market Distress / 18**
    The Baby Boom, the Business Cycle and Youthful Distress / 21
    The Issue of Scarring / 24
    Structure of Labor Market Distress among Youth / 26
    The Role of Education / 30
    Conclusion / 31

*Chapter 4*
**Disadvantaged Adults / 35**
    Disadvantaged Blacks—The Problem of Bifurcation / 39

Hispanics—Education and Acculturation / 41
Female-headed Families / 42
Conclusion / 43

*Chapter 5*
## Dislocated Workers / 45
Dislocation and Distress / 46
Industrial, Occupational and Regional Changes in the 1980s / 48
Conclusion / 55

*Chapter 6*
## Distressed Older Workers / 57
The Decrease in Labor Force Participation of Older Males / 60
Widowhood / 62
Conclusion / 63

*Chapter 7*
## Final Note / 65

*National Planning Association / 67*

*NPA Officers and Board of Trustees / 68*

*Recent NPA Publications / inside back cover*

TABLES AND FIGURES

1-1. Poverty Rate among Long-term Unemployed, by Family Status, Labor Force Participation and Duration, 1972-77 / **2**
1-2. Proportion of Total Variation in Annual Earnings "Explained" by Fixed Individual Characteristics and by Random Annual Variations for Male Household Heads, 1967-73 / **4**
2-1. U.S. Macroeconomic Performance Indicators, Actual 1961-82, Projected 1983-88 / **8**
Fig.
2-1. Proportion of Labor Force Age 16-24, 1960-2000 / **9**

Contents v

Fig.
2-2. Labor Force Participation Rates for Men and Women by Age, 1940-90 / **10**

Fig.
2-3. Simulation of Added Wage and Price Inflation Due to a 100 Percent Rise in Oil Prices Over the Course of One Year / **14**

Fig.
3-1. Job Tenure of Employed Males, 1978 / **19**

Fig.
3-2. Unemployment Rates by Age, Sex and Race, 1969 and 1978 / **20**

Fig.
3-3A. Unemployment Rates Corrected for the Business Cycle, 1947-80 / **22**

Fig.
3-3B. Ratios of Incomes of Younger Men (Women) to Those of Men (Women) Age 45 through 54, 1955-80 / **23**

3-1. Low Income Youth with Serious Unemployment or Nonemployment, by School and Family Status, 1978 / **25**

3-2. Civilian Employment-Population Ratios for Young Blacks, by Sex-Age Groups and by School and Central City Status, 1964 and 1978 / **28**

4-1. Distribution of Income for Families and Unrelated Individuals, 1965 and 1978 / **35**

Fig.
4-1. Distribution of the Number of Years in which a Male Household Head Had Annual Earnings in the Lowest Decile of Income Distribution for that Year, 1969-78 / **37**

4-2. Labor Market Performance of Female Household Heads, 1969-78 / **38**

4-3. Evidence of Economic Changes for Black Americans, 1949-79 / **40**

5-1. Economic Dislocation of "Mainstream" Workers, Age 22-64, for Occupations Experiencing Declining Total Employment, 1980 / **47**

5-2. Employment Levels and Changes by Industry, 1969-90 / **50**

5-3. Occupations Projected to Have Highest Growth by 1990, Rate Versus Number of Employees / **53**

Fig.
5-1. Per Capita Personal Income as a Percent of the U.S. Average, 1929-2000, BEA Regions / **54**

Fig.
6-1. Distribution of Retirement Ages, Retirement History Survey, 1969-79 / **58**

Fig.
6-2. Distribution of Retiree Earnings Around the Exempt Amount, Retirement History Survey, 1969-79 / **59**

6-1. Annual Average Percent of Unemployed in a Group Who Reported Continuous Unemployment of at Least Six Months, by Age and Sex, 1968 and 1978 / **60**

# A Statement by the Committee on New American Realities

American society faces continuing challenges to its efforts to provide adequate incomes, opportunities and security for all its members, including the least advantaged. Some of these challenges are the result of recent macroeconomic performance, while others arise from structural factors such as new technologies, intensifying foreign competition and an aging population. Yet others, such as persistent poverty among certain groups, are long-standing problems. But all require increasing attention if American society is to meet its own expectations.

The importance and difficulty of these challenges have led the Committee on New American Realities to focus on labor market, employment and human resource issues as one theme in its program of analysis and publication. This study by Professor Daniel Saks inaugurates the Committee's work in the area by providing an overview of labor market trends and conditions and by identifying the most critical problems likely to arise or persist in the 1980s. Further studies sponsored by the Committee will address in more detail particular problems and possible policy approaches.

Professor Saks identifies four groups of workers expected to face considerable difficulty in the labor market of the 1980s: youth who lack the skills, characteristics or opportunities to get started in the labor market; adults disadvantaged by life experiences or by cultural/personal circumstances; elderly workers (often with health problems) who have little earning power or other private income; and experienced workers in their prime years who are dislocated by technological or economic change. The problems of each group are quite different, and targeted policies must be designed for each.

Short periods of unemployment and low wages for some individuals are all too common in a dynamic market economy; unemployment insurance and income supplements are designed for such situations. But within the identified groups, low wages and unemployment will be chronic and concentrated, producing what the author calls "labor market distress." One of the most important points made by Professor Saks in this study is that such distress persists even in good economic times. He estimates that about 11 million workers, perhaps 10 percent of the labor force, were in distress in 1979, before the deep recession of the early 1980s. A strong economic recovery is essential to reduce labor market distress, but much will remain even if the recovery is strong.

The complexity of the distressed workers' situations can be highlighted by selected trends over the 1970s. Between 1969 and 1979, total employment increased by 21 million (or 29 percent), and female employment increased by 12 million (or 42 percent)—rates of increase far above those of earlier decades. By 1979, 48 percent of white women were employed, compared to only 40 percent in 1969. But over the same period, the percentage of black males who were employed fell from 73 to 65. And at least 5 million individual adults (often female heads of households) were in distress throughout the entire period—always in the labor market but typically in the lowest 10 percent of the earnings distribution. Thus, while the economy was creating jobs at unprecedented rates for large numbers of new workers, some critical groups were not even maintaining their proportional share of jobs, and millions of individuals were in continuing, unrelieved distress.

Demographic trends over the 1980s will be more favorable to workers: the post-World War II "baby boom" has now entered the labor force, so there will be fewer new competitors for jobs. However, the author points out that these favorable developments will be at least partially offset by the effects of slower economic growth (at least in the early 1980s), labor-displacing or educationally demanding technological change, increased immigration, and continuing international competition. It is impossible to predict the net effect of these conflicting trends on aggregate employment and wages, but it is clear that millions of individuals in the identified groups will remain in distress.

Professor Saks emphasizes that labor market distress seems to persist throughout the lives of some individuals. Many disadvantaged adults were youth with labor market problems earlier and will be elderly workers in distress later. It is unclear whether this is primarily because early labor market difficulties can "scar" an individual so that he or she never really recovers, or because some individuals begin their work careers with fixed characteristics that cause problems at all stages. But it is clear that the problems of distressed youth should be a major focus of public policy. If young people are given the basic skills they need to learn their jobs and if they have positive early job experiences, fewer of them will be in distress as adults and elderly workers.

Adults in persistent labor market distress can be helped by work and training programs and by programs that combine income maintenance with work incentives. Professor Saks points out that these programs have high costs, because they invariably result in public payments to workers who do not qualify for public assistance under traditional programs. However, he also points out that this additional transfer does benefit the working poor and their children, and can help distressed adults become productive and independent members of society.

The distress of older workers occurs at a stage in life when it is often too late for remedial action to be effective, especially when health problems are involved. The issue here is usually how to provide aid in the most humane and efficient way.

Professor Saks is moderately optimistic about the problems of dislocated workers and the employment effects of technological change and international competition, assuming the economy picks up. He cites evidence from the 1970s that most dislocated workers, even in declining occupations and industries, have found new jobs, although often at lower wages. The principal problems (especially for older workers and those accustomed to above average wages) occur where an entire geographic area suffers employment declines. Employment projections indicate that "high tech" employment will increase at a rapid proportional rate but from a small base; the largest numbers of new jobs will be in service occupations such as food preparation, trade and office work, where little specialized training is required. This suggests that large-scale retraining is neither the principal need nor a likely panacea in the labor market of the 1980s. The author concludes that displacement will be a significant source of labor market distress only if the economy is weak; in a strong economy, new jobs requiring similar skills (but perhaps paying lower wages) will be created to replace lost ones.*

These trends and the evidence from the 1970s concerning displaced workers are encouraging but not totally reassuring. As Professor Saks says, the growth of the economy and of jobs may not be as strong in the 1980s as in the previous decade; and geographically concentrated unemployment is a major problem in the United States. The type and pace of technological and economic change in the 1980s may be quite different from the recent past. Furthermore, there is no guarantee that the new jobs replacing the old will pay enough to those at the bottom of the scale to meet American society's expectations. Fundamental changes may be taking place in the structure of work and in the relationships between jobs and incomes; the nature and seriousness of such changes and their possible policy implications are subjects requiring further study.

The objective of this study is to identify and characterize some general problems, not to propose policy. The Committee does not necessarily endorse the recommendations or findings made by Professor Saks. But we believe the data and analyses he presents can help in understanding labor market and human problems of the 1980s. We are therefore pleased that it is being published by the National Planning Association as a report signed by its author.

---

* Lower wages for dislocated workers are not a necessary consequence of the dislocation. Steps should be taken to assure that the economy reasonably maintains a dislocated worker's standard of living.—**Glenn E. Watts**

# Members of the Committee on New American Realities Signing the Statement

JOHN S. REED
*Chairman;* Vice Chairman, Citibank, N.A.

J.F. BENNETT
Director and Senior Vice President, Exxon Corporation

JAMES B. BOOE
Executive Vice President, Communications Workers of America, AFL-CIO

KENNETH J. BROWN
President, Graphic Communications International Union

HUGH CULLMAN
Chairman and Chief Executive Officer, Philip Morris U.S.A., and Group Executive Vice President, Philip Morris, Inc.

RICHARD M. CYERT
President, Carnegie Mellon University

DONALD F. EPHLIN
Vice President–International Union, United Auto Workers of America

MURRAY H. FINLEY
President, Amalgamated Clothing & Textile Workers' Union

THEODORE GEIGER
Distinguished Research Professor of Intersocietal Relations, School of Foreign Service, Georgetown University

JEROME S. GORE
Chairman and Chief Executive Officer, Hartmarx Corporation

DALE HATHAWAY
Consultants International

R.J. HILDRETH
Managing Director, Farm Foundation

CHARLES S. JOHNSON
Vice President, Finance and Treasurer, Pioneer Hi-Bred International

EDWARD G. JORDAN
President, The American College

RICHARD C. KAUTZ
Chairman, Grain Processing Corporation

JAMES E. LIEBIG
Vice President, Human Resources, Schneider National Inc.

CHARLES MARSHALL
Chairman and Chief Executive Officer, American Bell

WILLIAM J. McDONOUGH
Executive Vice President and Chief Financial Officer, The First National Bank of Chicago

JOHN MILLER
Vice Chairman, National Planning Association

RUDOLPH OSWALD
Director, Department of Economic Research, AFL-CIO

DEAN P. PHYPERS
Senior Vice President, IBM Corporation

MARSHALL ROBINSON
President, Russell Sage Foundation

RICHARD M. ROSENBERG
Vice Chairman, Wells Fargo Bank

ROBERT L. SHAFER
Vice President-Government Relations, Pfizer Inc.

LAUREN K. SOTH
Register and Tribune Syndicate

WALTER STERLING SURREY
Senior Partner, Surrey and Morse

ALEXANDER C. TOMLINSON
President, National Planning Association

J.C. TURNER
General President, International Union of Operating Engineers

*GLENN E. WATTS
President, Communications Workers of America, AFL-CIO

RALPH S. YOHE
Editor, *Wisconsin Agriculturist*

*The opinions expressed and the recommendations presented in the Committee Statement are solely those of the individual members of the Committee on New American Realities whose signatures are offered hereto and do not represent the views of the National Planning Association or its staff. Committee members' agreement or disagreement with specific points of the Statement may be expressed in signed footnotes.*

---

*See footnote to the Statement.

# Acknowledgments

This report is partially based on work supported by grants from the Rockefeller Foundation and the U.S. German Marshall Fund. Much of the research reported below was initiated and supported by the National Commission for Employment Policy when the author was Director, 1980–81. The author wishes to thank members of the Committee on New American Realities and the staff of the National Planning Association for comments and help with this report. Larry Ruff, Research Director of the NAR, made numerous improvements in an earlier manuscript. Louise Russell, Sar Levitan and Eli Ginsberg also had many helpful criticisms and insights on an earlier draft.

# Chapter 1
# *Introduction*

There is no doubt that strong economic growth is the most important source of rising living standards and economic opportunities for workers in general and even for those at the bottom of the economic ladder. However, the evidence is clear that some groups containing large numbers of individuals do poorly in the labor market even in good economic times. This report analyses the dimensions of labor market distress likely to persist even if a strong economic recovery does occur.

No one knows precisely how the labor market will develop during the 1980s or which workers will be in distress. The difficulty of prediction is illustrated by pointing out that only one of the three critical economic events of the 1970s could have been confidently predicted at the outset of that decade: the coming of age of the baby-boom generation and its absorption into the labor force. The other two major events surprised many experts: the doubling of international trade's share of the U.S. economy with the competition this posed for domestic producers; and the trebling of energy prices with the consequent problems of economic adjustment. Long-term trends that were expected to continue included the decentralization of the cities, the rising labor force participation of mothers, the increase in female-headed families, the relative decline of manufacturing employment, the shift out of blue-collar occupations, the increase in school attainment of the workforce, and the strong economic growth of the Sunbelt.

The 1980s too will be affected by continued long-term trends, some reasonably predictable special events and some unsettling surprises. While this report is not an exact prediction of labor market distress, it offers a prognosis based on what is known about the past and what is most likely for the future. Its theme is that labor market distress over the 1980s is likely to be concentrated in particular groups and places.

## Definition of Distress in the Labor Market

Two categories of labor market distress are discussed in this study. The first is the distress of *disadvantaged workers* whose "normal" earnings—the level of income they have come to rely on and to expect, given their training, experience and situation—are too low to raise their families above the official poverty line. The other category is more difficult to define and refers to the distress of *dislocated workers* who suffer a sudden and relatively long-term drop in earnings below their "normal" level. Although these dislocations do not always or even usually result in poverty, society may still feel that the resulting distress requires special help.

**Disadvantaged workers.** The disadvantaged workers to be considered here are those whose earnings, even when they work regularly, cannot provide their families' subsistence. This category does not include people who are not expected to be in the labor force because of ill health, retirement or other demands on their time.

If the official U.S. government poverty threshold ($7,412 for a nonfarm family of four in 1979[1]) is used as a measure of the income required for a family's subsistence, then the number of disadvantaged workers can be quantified. Of the 168 million Americans 15 or more years of age in 1979 (the most recent year in which labor markets were buoyant), almost 17 million were living in poor families.[2] About 10 million of these reported they were not in the labor force because they were keeping house (36 percent), ill or disabled (27 percent), in school (17 percent), or retired (16 percent).[3] Of concern here are the other almost 7 million poor with some labor force attachment, representing 40 percent of poor youth and adults. Also of concern are perhaps an additional 4 million

Table 1-1. *Poverty Rate among Long-term Unemployed, by Family Status, Labor Force Participation and Duration, 1972-77*

| Family Status[1] and Labor Force Participation[2] | Percent of Workers in Each Group in Poverty by Duration of Unemployment (Weeks) | | | | | All Unemployed |
|---|---|---|---|---|---|---|
| | 0 | 1-4 | 5-14 | 15-26 | 27+ | |
| Husbands in labor force full-time (36 million[3]) | 2.6 | 4.2 | 6.4 | 12.1 | 26.7 | 11.0 |
| Wives in labor force full-time (17 million[3]) | 1.9 | 1.7 | 2.1 | 3.2 | 8.0 | 3.8 |
| Female heads in labor force full-time (4 million[3]) | 8.7 | 16.1 | 21.0 | 35.1 | 55.6 | 33.3 |
| Husbands in labor force part-time (3 million[3]) | 9.4 | 13.6 | 19.1 | 25.1 | 33.8 | 20.9 |
| Wives in labor force part-time (8 million[3]) | 4.9 | 8.0 | 7.1 | 8.8 | 12.4 | 8.0 |

1 Husbands and wives are in husband-wife families. Female heads in the labor force part time are not shown because the sample size was too small (less than 1 million in 1977).
2 "Part-time" means less than 48 weeks per year; "full-time" means 48 or more weeks per year.
3 Estimated size of group in 1977.

Source: Special report for the National Commission on Employment and Unemployment Statistics, *Counting the Labor Force* (Bureau of Labor Statistics, 1979), p. 67.

people with at least a week of labor force participation in 1979 who would have lived in poverty had it not been for food stamps and cash transfer payments from government programs.[4]

These 11 million disadvantaged workers can best be described as "earnings poor": whether because of market failure, chance or choice, they did not earn enough to bring their families out of poverty. The hope is that effective labor market policies might raise such workers above poverty by improving their productivity and opportunities so that their subsistence comes from what they produce rather than from government transfers.

It is important to note that the principal problem for the earnings poor is not always lack of employment. As Table 1-1 demonstrates, from 1972 to 1977, only 26.7 percent of husbands and 55.6 percent of female household heads in the labor force full time who suffered at least 27 weeks of unemployment in a year were poor; the rest of the families had income sufficient to keep them above the poverty level despite long-term unemployment. On the other hand, 2.6 percent of husbands and 8.7 percent of female household heads who worked all year were poor, presumably because of low wages and too few hours of work.

**Dislocated workers.** While earnings below the official poverty level are an important measure of labor market distress, another relates to unanticipated declines in earnings below normal levels. Such a decline due to changing market conditions or techniques of production can be described as "dislocation," which becomes a source of distress if continued long enough even if the family is not pushed below the poverty level.

To judge the importance and severity of the dislocation phenomenon and to consider the appropriate remedial actions, it is necessary to know the frequency and magnitude of its occurrence. If large year-to-year fluctuations in individual earnings are normal, different policies are required than if they are rare. If dislocation tends, on average, to be rapidly self-correcting rather than long lived, there is less cause for general concern. To decide what the facts are, data on the earnings of individuals over time are needed.

Based on data for 1967 to 1973, Lillard and Willis have calculated the variation in annual earnings among male household heads, using a statistical procedure that distinguishes permanent from transitory variations.[5] Their analysis explains an individual's normal annual earnings in terms of race and three sets of factors: (1) years of schooling and on-the-job training and experience—the "human capital" that should make workers more productive and give them higher earnings because schools and employers have either "sorted" them or taught them useful skills; (2) other fixed measurable variables such as details of the individual's employment experience, marital status and labor market size and region; and (3) fixed but unmeasured factors, such as motivation, intelligence, social or family contacts, and presence, which cannot be precisely defined or measured but affect an individual's productivity or ability to get and keep a job. Year-to-year variations in an individual's earnings from the normal level predicted for him on the basis of these fixed individual factors can be attributed to labor market dislocations (for negative variations) or good luck (for positive variations)—although, of course, choice as well as chance is involved in determining these year-to-year variations.

Some relevant results from the Lillard-Willis study are summarized in Table 1-2. Differences in years of education and experience were particularly important in accounting for variations in annual earnings over the 1967-73 period, explaining 29 percent of the variation for whites and 41 percent for blacks. Other fixed individual factors, measured and unmeasured, accounted for 42 percent of the variation for whites and 40 percent for blacks. In total, fixed individual variables, rather than transitory "random" events, explained 71 percent of the variation in annual earnings for whites and 81 percent for blacks.

In very rough terms (and assuming that negative and positive variations were equally likely), this result means that if a male household head had annual earnings in any year from 1967 to 1973 below the average for his race, the odds were about 2.4 to 1 ($71 \div 29$) for whites and 4.2 to 1 ($81 \div 19$) for blacks that relatively fixed individual factors, rather than temporary labor market dislocations, were the principal causes.

The Lillard-Willis study also indicates that variations in earnings that are not explained by fixed individual factors did not last long, on average, during 1967-73. The statistical analysis indicated that only about 40 percent of any random variation in annual earnings persisted

Table 1-2. *Proportion of Total Variation in Annual Earnings "Explained" by Fixed Individual Characteristics and by Random Annual Variations for Male Household Heads, 1967-73*

| Explanatory Factors | Whites | Blacks |
| --- | --- | --- |
| Fixed over period | | |
|   Education and experience | 29% | 41% |
|   Other measured factors | 18 | 18 |
|   Unmeasured fixed factors | 24 | 22 |
|   Total | 71% | 81% |
| Random annual variations | 29 | 19 |
|   Total | 100% | 100% |

Source: Lee A. Lillard and Robert J. Willis, "Dynamic Aspects of Earning Mobility," *Econometrica*, Vol. 46, No. 5 (September 1978), pp. 985-1012.

from year to year. This means, for example, that if a worker's income in one year were 50 percent below the level that would have been normal given his education, experience and other fixed personal factors, that income would be only 20 percent (0.4 × 50 percent) below normal the next year, and only 8 percent (0.4 × 0.4 × 50 percent) below normal the third year.

In summary, then, the Lillard-Willis study indicates that no more than 20 to 30 percent of below average earnings in any single year may be due to short-term dislocations. Furthermore, the effects of these dislocations on any individual worker fade rapidly, so that the typical earnings of individuals over a period of several years are not greatly affected by short-term dislocations. Because the unemployment insurance system is designed to deal with much of the shorter-term earnings loss, this study deals only with the distress caused by longer-term labor market dislocations as well as that caused by the relatively fixed factors that keep an individual's normal earnings too low.

## Classifying Causes and Solutions of Distress

To organize a study of likely sources of future labor market distress, it is useful to focus on groups born in the same decade and hence at similar stages in their life cycles. The people in such a cohort, or generation, share significant characteristics and experiences. For example, because cohort members compete more with each other than with members of other cohorts for schools, jobs and other resources, the unusually large cohort born in the 1950s will face special conditions throughout its life. Cohorts share experiences such as wars, depressions, economic shifts, advances in knowledge, and fads in education, which affect a generation's attitudes toward economic decisions and the resources at its disposal. For example, cohorts coming of age during periods of high and persistent unemployment may lose opportunities for labor market experiences that would have made them more productive later in their lives.

But not all members of a cohort are born into the same situations, share the same experiences or are affected equally by their experiences. Such differences generate special problems for some individuals because of discrimination, background, location, occupation, or industry of employment. These "structural" problems are not shared with their cohort as a whole.

The approach of this report is to focus on four groups experiencing structural problems at different stages of their life cycles: (1) disadvantaged youth having trouble breaking into the labor market; (2) disadvantaged adults whose normal earnings are insufficient to bring their families out of poverty; (3) dislocated middle-aged workers who have difficulty adjusting to changes in the labor market; and (4) distressed older workers whose poor health or other impediments make them low earners or jobless with little or no retirement income. Each group will be discussed separately, although together they may be seen as a panorama of the consecutive stages of labor market distress in America.

Before turning to an analysis of the four groups in distress, certain features of the economic environment of the 1980s will be described in the next chapter. The groups in distress in the labor market are inevitably larger in a weak economy, and hence often more can be done for them by improving economic growth than by targeting programs. Similarly, special programs are likely to work better in a tighter labor market where workers who have been given help are more likely to find jobs. The weak economy of the early 1980s exacerbates almost every economic problem except inflation—and even that may revive in the longer run. It should be kept in mind that the frame of reference for this report is the labor market of the late 1970s, the last time anything like a high employment labor market existed. That is why the data appearing here consciously stop at the end of the seventies. The high general unemployment levels caused by the severe recession of the early 1980s were grafted on top of the structural problems discussed in this report.

The emphasis here is on the dimensions of labor market distress and its causes rather than on an evaluation of policies to deal with such distress.[6] However, this report is meant as a backdrop to future policy discussions, and the final chapter briefly notes some broad policy directions.

## Notes

1 U.S. Bureau of the Census, *Money Income and Poverty Status of Families and Persons in the United States: 1979 (Advanced Report)*, Consumer Income Series P-60, No. 125 (October 1980), p. 38.

2 Ibid., p. 33. Income in kind is not counted in these statistics.

3 Ibid. Of course, in the presence of different policies and incentives and better labor market opportunities, some of these people would enter the labor force.

4 Robert Taggart, "The Hardship Consequences of Labor Market Problems" (Center for Social Policy Studies, George Washington University, June 17, 1982).

5 Lee A. Lillard and Robert J. Willis, "Dynamic Aspects of Earning Mobility," *Econometrica*, Vol. 46, No. 5 (September 1978), pp. 985–1012.

6 For a discussion of the role of training programs in relieving distress and dislocation, readers should consult the author's forthcoming monograph from which some of the material for this report was also drawn: Daniel H. Saks, *Trainfare: Federal Training Programs for the Disadvantaged and Dislocated Worker in the Eighties* (Washington: Brookings Institution, forthcoming 1984).

*Chapter 2*
# The Labor Market in the 1980s

The economic environment facing distressed workers in the 1980s is the product of offsetting trends. The potential labor force will be growing only two-thirds as fast in the 1980s as it did in the 1970s, which should reduce competition for jobs on the supply side of the labor market. The demand side, however, is likely to be very weak, particularly for those workers most at risk of distress; the anti-inflation policies early in the decade have induced high unemployment, and the hoped-for growth of investment later in the 1980s—if it develops—will accelerate dislocation through technological change.

**The Macroeconomic Environment**

While the decade is not off to a good start, it is still young. Economic adjustments, including reallocation of capital and labor, incorporation of productivity-enhancing technology, reorganization of economic activities, and other needed changes, take place with least resistance in a buoyant economy. Without strong growth to create new jobs for dislocated workers and to upgrade unskilled workers, there will be more resistance to competition from abroad, inadequate public and private investment, and attempts to protect and encourage uneconomical activities. A spiral of declining growth is easier to set in motion than to stop.

Long-term economic projections can be illuminating if they are treated cautiously. They can provide a consistent way to assess the effects of reasonable assumptions about government policy, productivity growth and other variables that are inherently uncertain. Table 2-1 displays the February 1983 baseline forecast of the Congressional Budget Office, which indicates weak growth in GNP and high unemployment for the first half of the decade. The recent tax cuts and declining inflation are expected to encourage investment and growth eventually; the unemployment rate is projected to decrease slowly from its peak in 1983–84, reaching in the late 1980s levels that still exceed those typical of the 1960s and '70s. Inflation is forecast to decline over the 1980s, but not to return to the low levels of the early 1960s. Furthermore, CBO warns that these long-term projections may not fully reflect the adverse effects of the budget deficits they foresee. While it is already

Table 2-1. **U.S. Macroeconomic Performance Indicators, Actual 1961-82, Projected 1983-88**

| | Average Annual Growth Rate in | | Average Rate of Unemployment |
|---|---|---|---|
| | Real GNP | GNP Deflator | |
| 1961-65 | 4.7% | 1.6% | 5.5% |
| 1966-70 | 3.2 | 4.2 | 3.9 |
| 1971-75 | 2.6 | 6.5 | 6.1 |
| 1976-80 | 2.0 | 7.2 | 6.8 |
| 1981 | 1.9 | 9.1 | 7.6 |
| 1982 | -1.8 | 6.0 | 9.7 |
| 1983 | 2.1 | 4.6 | 10.6 |
| 1984 | 4.7 | 4.7 | 9.8 |
| 1985 | 4.1 | 4.7 | 9.0 |
| 1986 | 3.7 | 4.3 | 8.4 |
| 1987 | 3.5 | 3.9 | 8.0 |
| 1988 | 3.5 | 3.8 | 7.5 |

Sources: Actual rates calculated from *1983 Economic Report of the President,* Table B-2. Projections from *Baseline Budget Projections for Fiscal Years 1984-1988* (U.S. Congress, Congressional Budget Office, February 1983), p. 6.

evident that CBO underestimated the strength of the early stages of the current recovery, monetary policy may yet choke off this growth.

The following sections present a more detailed analysis of the composition of demand and supply and their interactions in the labor market. These interactions will determine the economic environment in which labor market distress will occur and the magnitude of that distress.

**The Supply Side**

The supply of labor can be defined as the amount of (quality-adjusted) person years of labor the population is willing to provide at a given level of compensation and is largely determined by the number and characteristics of working-age people. In the 1980s, the most important supply-side event will be the decline in young new entrants into the labor force. As Figure 2-1 shows, the proportion of the labor force between the ages of 16 and 24, which increased dramatically over the 1970s, is projected to decrease over the 1980s to the level of 1970. The baby-boom generation has now passed into the labor force, only to be replaced by the "baby-bust" generation of the late 1960s and '70s.

The implications for youth of this decline in young labor force entrants will be discussed in the next chapter. The implication for the economy overall is that the labor force will grow slowly because of fewer new entrants. The changing age composition of that workforce will have a disappointing impact on the overall growth rate of the potential output of the economy. Reduced growth in the groups (especially young women) with the fastest rising labor force participation rates will offset the output gains from a more experienced workforce. Thus, the aging of the workforce itself during the first half of the 1980s will induce offsetting quantity and quality effects.

Another important supply-side factor in the labor market of the 1980s is the continued growth of women's share of the labor force. This is the continuation of a long-term trend and is not likely to be reversed over the decade. As Figure 2-2 shows, each cohort of women born this century has had higher labor force participation rates at every age than have earlier cohorts.[1] The shift of women from home to market work is a consequence of the long-term and continuing rise of real wages, the changing technology of housekeeping and the extension of compulsory public school attendance for children.[2]

The productivity of the labor force, which is determined in large part by its education and training, is another important dimension of labor supply. Despite the slowdown in labor productivity growth during the 1970s, Denison estimates that education and training, particularly at the high school and college levels, contributed 0.88 percentage points per year to the growth of labor productivity during 1973-76,

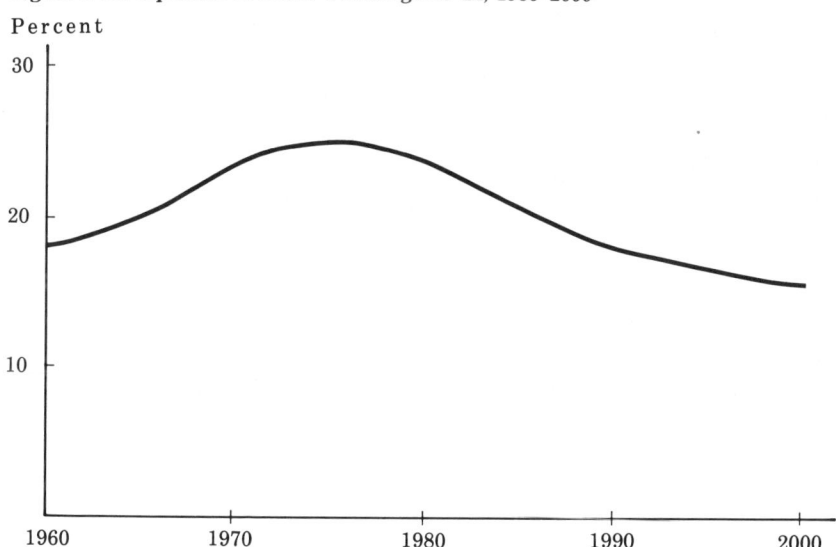

Figure 2-1. Proportion of Labor Force Age 16-24, 1960-2000

Source: Nestor E. Terleckyj, Martin K. Holdrich and David M. Levy, *U.S. Economic Growth to 2000* (Washington: National Planning Association, December 1982).

*Figure 2-2. Labor Force Participation Rates for Men and Women by Age, 1940–90*

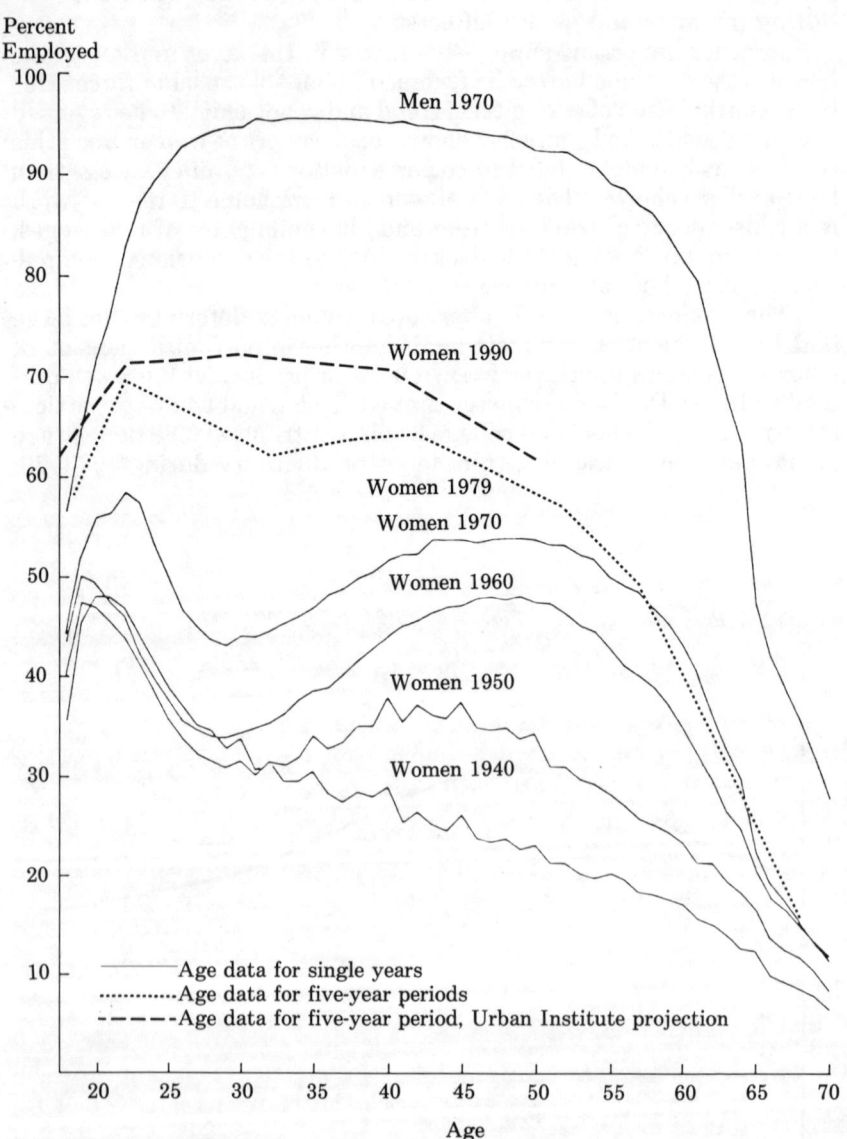

Source: George Masnick and Mary Jo Bane, *The Nation's Families: 1960–1990* (Cambridge, Mass.: Joint Center for Urban Studies of MIT and Harvard University, 1980). Reproduced with permission.

over one-third a percentage point more than in the 1948-73 period.[3] Because most of the workforce now has a high school education (the proportion with less than a high school education has fallen by at least two-thirds since 1948), any further gains from education will have to come from increasing that proportion of the workforce with some college (one-third in the late 1970s) or by improving the quality of education. However, the economic returns to investments in college education—the present value of the higher earnings versus the costs (including foregone earnings) of the education—appear to have fallen during the 1970s because of the high college enrollment of the baby-boom generation and the decline in the relative demand for professionals and managers.[4] Coupled with the reduction in wage premiums for many skilled workers that occurred during the 1970s, this is likely to reduce college enrollment rates and investment in training during the 1980s, resulting in slower gains in labor productivity from education and training than in the past.

With potential employment growing at relatively low rates and with less productivity growth expected from education and training, the remaining factor that could produce large increases in effective labor supply is the "wild card" of immigration.[5] The size and composition of immigration will determine whether labor supply will grow as slowly as indicated above and who among the native population will win and lose.

Legal immigration to this country peaked in the first decade of the century at an annual rate of 10.4 per thousand of the U.S. population and fell to a low of 0.4 per thousand during the 1930s.[6] It has been rising since, and during 1975-78 was 2.2 per thousand annually. Migrants are generally self-selected to be above average in economic performance (more able, aggressive and entrepreneurial), given their level of education and experience. Although legal migrants tend to be unskilled and initially to have lower earnings than similar native workers, within 11 to 15 years after arrival their earnings exceed those of similar domestic workers.

Illegal migration, especially from Mexico, has increased sharply in the past two decades, largely in response to changes in the immigration laws in the mid 1960s that limited the number of legal migrants and stopped programs allowing the temporary migration of agricultural workers. Although illegal migrants are obviously hard to identify, best estimates of the stock of illegal immigrants in 1980 were between 3.5 million and 6 million (or about 5 percent of the labor force), with almost half coming from Mexico. Apparently, these illegal immigrants frequently go back and forth to their native countries. They appear to be mostly unskilled workers employed at slightly better than the minimum wage, on average.

Of interest here is whether such migration contributes to labor market distress for native workers. It is clear that illegal migrants are most competitive with low skilled domestic workers. Johnson has calculated the hypothetical consequences of increasing the stock of unskilled migrants from 4 million to 5 million, on the assumption (and this is consistent with the evidence) that an increased supply of low skilled workers would lower the wages of all low skilled workers but would cause little unemployment.[7] He estimated that domestic low skilled workers would receive wages that are lower by about 4 percent and would lose about 3.5 percent of their total income; GNP would increase by about 0.5 percent; and the incomes of high skilled workers and of property owners—whose labor and capital is complementary with unskilled workers in production—would each rise by about 0.5 percent.

It is not easy to protect unskilled workers from the wage-depressing effects of illegal immigration without causing other problems. Applying sanctions against employers who hire illegal migrants is likely to increase the employment difficulties of legal migrants and citizens of Hispanic origin, further depressing their wages and increasing the wages of non-Hispanic unskilled workers. Hence, income distribution issues are involved here among the unskilled workers as well as between them and other groups. In any case, immigration policy appears to be moving toward further restriction of such immigration, which should at least provide some gains for non-Hispanic distressed workers.

The final issue to be discussed in this section is the impact on labor supply of the recent cuts in personal income taxes. Assuming that the ordinary rules of economic behavior continue to hold, labor supply will not be greatly affected. Economic theory makes no prediction about the total impact on labor supply of a tax cut because there are two offsetting consequences: net wages are higher, tending to induce more work; but the higher wages make workers richer, and hence they tend to consume more leisure. The percentage change in aggregate hours of work resulting from a 1 percent change in wages at the margin is estimated to be about 0.15.[8] Thus, the currently legislated reduction in the marginal personal income tax rate of 1.7 percentage points between 1980 and 1984 for the average taxpayer would increase labor supply by 0.25 percent in total over the first half of the decade. There may be, of course, some changes in the composition of the labor force because the marginal tax rate reductions may have greater impact on the labor supply of wives and on the more highly educated workers in higher tax brackets. But these tax cuts do relatively little for lower paid workers near the distress level and furthermore are partially offset by higher Social Security taxes.

**The Demand Side**

The news from the supply side is, on balance, good for distressed workers: decreased competition for jobs that should increase pressures for rising real wages. Unfortunately, over the first half of the decade, anti-inflation policies will weaken labor demand much more than demographic changes will decrease supply.

The relation between inflation and unemployment is a subject of some debate among economists, and an extended discussion will not be undertaken here. There is evidence that higher unemployment will reduce the rate of inflation, but at tremendous cost in terms of lost output.[9] An extra one million people may have to be out of work for two years in order to reduce inflation by only 1 percentage point.

Much of the increase in inflation in the 1970s was a result of the Organization of Petroleum Exporting Countries (OPEC) oil price rises. Since such commodity price shocks take as long as five years to work through all the intermediate goods prices in the economy, inflation induced by the last oil price rise will be positive but declining through the early 1980s. Figure 2-3 shows a simulation based on data from recent decades indicating that a 100 percent increase in oil prices adds 2.5 percentage points to the inflation rate the year after it occurs; the effects fade away over the next several years, but generate subsequent echoes as workers try to maintain their real incomes. The fading away of the effects of the oil price rises of the late 1970s, combined with recent oil price declines and the extraordinarily high current levels of unemployment, mean that the inflation rate will decline through mid decade if economic policy maintains its present course. Current policy accepts high unemployment as the price for reducing inflation. Further, if the clash between a stimulative fiscal policy and a restrictive monetary policy continues, it will keep interest rates high and restrict expenditures on consumer durables and other forms of investment.

This is bad news for distressed workers because the costs of higher national unemployment are not shared equally among the population. Clark and Summers found that, during 1974, one-half of the total weeks of unemployment was due to spells lasting three or more months; 73 percent of all unemployment was experienced by individuals who suffered 15 or more weeks of joblessness; and 40 percent of all unemployment was experienced by the 2.5 percent of the labor force who suffered more than six months of unemployment.[10] Thus, unemployment is a mixture of many people having short periods of joblessness and a few people with long periods.

Furthermore, for every percentage point rise in the unemployment rate, the *average* income of stable families with traditional labor force attachment goes down 1 percent—but the effects are unevenly distributed.[11] For poor white husband-wife families, the decline is twice as large as for the average family; for poor black husband-wife families, the effect is three and one-half times as large. During the late 1970s, half of these earnings declines were offset by public transfer programs like unemployment insurance and food stamps, but such help has diminished under recent budget cuts. Further, the lost labor market experience of the unemployed may lower their permanent earnings (see the discussion in the next chapter).

If excessive unemployment is costly, especially to poorer and less skilled workers, what is a reasonable target for unemployment? Or,

*Figure 2-3. Simulation of Added Wage and Price Inflation Due to a 100 Percent Rise in Oil Prices Over the Course of One Year*

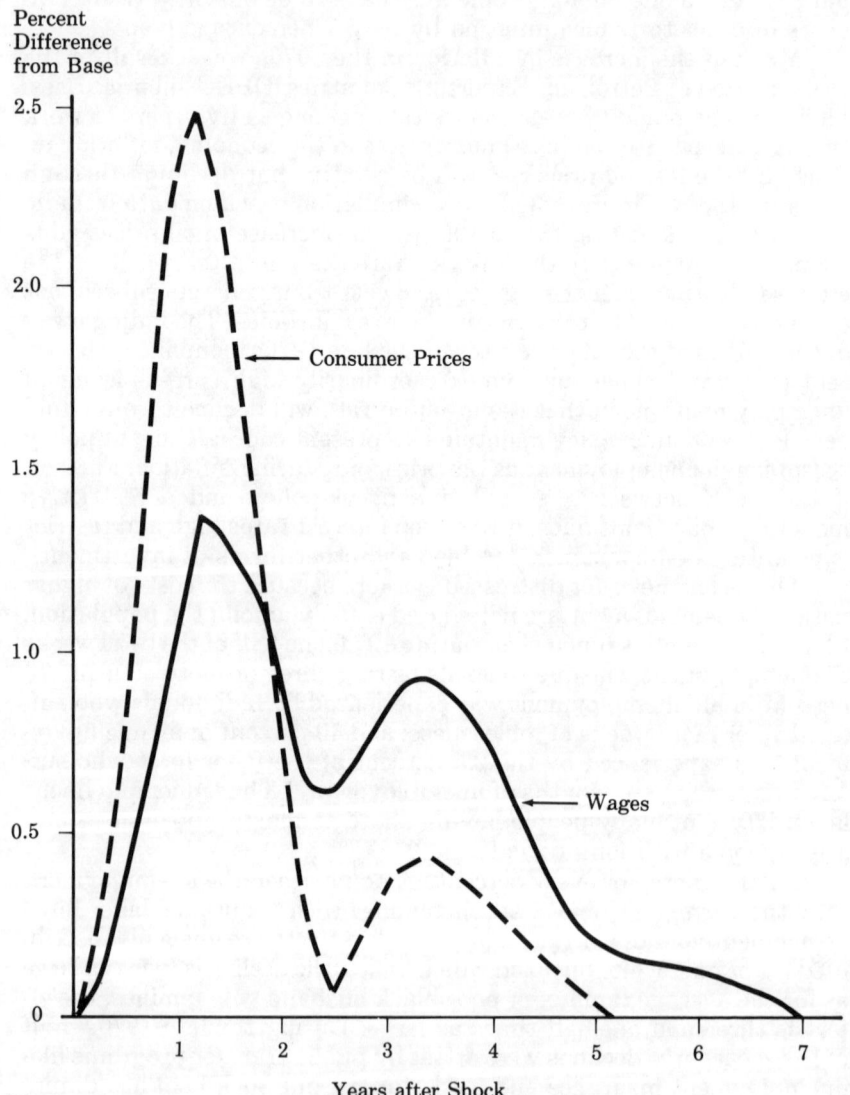

Source: Stephen G. Cecchetti, David S. McClain, Michael J. McKee, and Daniel H. Saks, "OPEC II and the Wage-Price Spiral," ed. Richard Zeckhauser, *What Role for Government* (Durham, N.C.: Duke University Press, 1983).

more precisely, what is the lowest unemployment rate that will not induce increased inflation? This can be called the high employment or "target" unemployment rate.

Unfortunately, the target unemployment rate is neither stable nor ever directly or clearly observed. It is, in fact, a function of many factors. For one thing, the shift of the labor force toward groups with higher "normal" unemployment rates—for example, youth who are more often unemployed while looking for better jobs—tends to raise the target rate above its level of earlier years. According to Russell's calculations, by 1980 the rising proportion of high unemployment labor force components had raised the target unemployment rate by almost half a point over the 4.14 percent it would have been given a labor force with the same components as that in 1957.[12] This trend will reverse over the 1980s, however, and the target unemployment rate corrected for demographic composition will decline by at least one-fourth and perhaps as much as one-third a percentage point. So unemployment will be considerably higher than the target over the 1980s.

Inflation is not just a labor market phenomenon: when unemployment was reduced to 5.8 percent in 1979, it was tight plant capacity rather than a tight labor market that constrained further improvement and tended to push prices up. It is unclear why this gap between product and labor markets developed during the 1970s or why, during the late 1960s, it was the labor market rather than product markets that constrained economic expansion. As recently as 1973, product and labor markets simultaneously reached levels of tightness associated with high employment. It seems likely that in the 1980s, however, low investment due to high real interest rates in the early part of the decade has exacerbated the problem. Indeed, such underinvestment may be one of the mechanisms by which high unemployment in one period reduces the ability of the economy to reach lower levels of unemployment in later periods—an affect that might be called the "structuralization" of unemployment. Another mechanism may be that workers lose skills from not using them while employers do not redesign jobs to use more effectively the available labor force.

Whether the economy could have been put on a better growth path with looser monetary and tighter fiscal policies during the early part of the 1980s can never be known. However, a real GNP growth rate of 2.5–3.0 percent per year would be needed simply to maintain a given unemployment rate in the face of a growing labor force. Each extra percentage point of real GNP growth above this reduces unemployment only about one-half a point because of increased labor productivity, longer work weeks for employed workers and reentry of people into the labor force in response to improved opportunities. Even a 5 percent per year GNP growth rate would reduce unemployment only about 1 percentage point each year. Therefore, weak labor demand will probably persist well past the middle of the decade, offsetting the favorable supply-side trends discussed above. The best hope is that capital accumulation will increase during the second half of the decade, raising the wages and employment of labor needed to operate the new capital.

The composition of labor demand as well as the rate of economic growth are important in affecting the labor market. Most of the compositional issues are deferred until Chapter 5, "Dislocated Workers." However, it is worth emphasizing here that there will be significant changes in the composition of labor demand as the trend away from manufacturing and toward the service sector continues; this does not mean that manufacturing output will decline, only that the proportion (and perhaps even the absolute numbers) of the workforce engaged in manufacturing will decline. Furthermore, changes in the distribution of job skill requirements in the U.S. economy between 1960 and 1976 appear to have caused a decrease in both low *and* high skill jobs and an increase in jobs requiring middle level skills[13]; this may account for the narrowing of wage differentials over the recent decade. These changes have implications for the types of education and training programs needed to match workers' skills to jobs and for the possible need for worker adjustment-assistance programs.

## Conclusion

The prospects for distress in the labor market are decreased when the incoming supply of low skilled workers is less and when the labor market is tighter so that the unemployed can more readily find new jobs. Supply conditions in the 1980s are generally favorable, but are likely to be more than offset by poor demand conditions. Certainly the beginning of the decade is not auspicious for hopes that strong demand might encourage investment in both physical and human capital. But there is always great uncertainty about the course of macroeconomic policies. This report focuses on the distress that is likely to remain even if a strong economic recovery occurs. It is based on conditions like those in the relatively tight labor market of the late 1970s. However, even if a strong recovery were to occur, it appears that unemployment will be higher than in the late 1970s; thus, much of what follows should be seen as an optimistic estimate of the degree of labor market distress.

### Notes

1 George Masnick and Mary Jo Bane, *The Nation's Families: 1960-1990* (Cambridge, Mass.: Joint Center for Urban Studies of MIT and Harvard University, 1980), p. 71.

2 One uncertainty of female labor force participation needs to be addressed: the interaction between cohort size and the labor force participation of women. Wachter projects a sharp decline during the 1980s in the growth of labor force participation of young women age 20 to 34. See Michael L. Wachter, "The Labor Market and Immigration: the Outlook

# Notes

for the 1980s," in Interagency Task Force on Immigration Policy, *Staff Report Companion Papers* (August 1979), pp. 163-234. He reasons that larger cohorts have lower wages because members of a cohort compete with one another in the labor market and thus drive wages down. Young families respond to lower income by fielding more workers. Since the baby-bust cohort is small, its wages will be relatively high and, according to this theory, the pressure on young wives to work will be less intense (and they might also be expected to have higher fertility rates). However, rising real wages for women in the smaller cohort may pull them into the labor force and reduce their fertility. See William P. Butz and Michael P. Ward, "Baby Boom and Baby Bust: A New View," *American Demographics*, Vol. 1 (September 1979), pp. 11-17. On balance, there seems to be little reason to expect major changes from past trends in the growing labor force participation of women.

3 Edward F. Denison, *Accounting for Slower Economic Growth, The United States in the 1970s* (Washington: Brookings Institution, 1979), pp. 42-47, 91-102.

4 For discussion and more extensive references, see Richard B. Freeman, "The Evolution of the American Labor Market, 1948-80," in Martin Feldstein, ed., *The American Economy in Transition* (Chicago: University of Chicago Press, 1980), pp. 349-414. Discussion of demand factors in the early 1970s can be found in Stephen P. Dresch, "Demography, Technology, and Higher Education: Toward a Former Model of Educational Adaptation," *Journal of Political Economy*, Vol. 83 (June 1975), pp. 535-569.

5 Another potential source of labor supply is from older workers. While they might respond to changes in Social Security regulations, there is reason to believe such changes will be phased in slowly and that the labor force participation of older workers will continue to decline or at least not increase. See Chapter 6, "Distressed Older Workers."

6 The following material is from a very useful survey of the subject by Barry R. Chiswick, "Immigrants in the U.S. Labor Market," *Annals of the American Academy of Political and Social Science*, Vol. 460 (March 1982), pp. 64-72.

7 George E. Johnson, "The Labor Market Effects of Immigration into the United States: A Summary of the Conceptual Issues," in Interagency Task Force on Immigration, *Staff Report Companion Papers* (August 1979).

8 Don Fullerton, "On the Possibility of an Inverse Relationship Between Tax Rates and Government Revenues," National Bureau of Economic Research Working Paper No. 467 (April 1980), p. 19.

9 For instance, see Stephen G. Cecchetti, David S. McClain, Michael J. McKee, and Daniel H. Saks, "OPEC II and the Wage-Price Spiral," ed. Richard Zeckhauser, *What Role for Government* (Durham, N.C.: Duke University Press, 1983).

10 Kim B. Clark and Lawrence H. Summers, "Labor Market Dynamics and Unemployment: A Reconsideration," *Brookings Papers on Economic Activity*, No. 1 (1979), pp. 13-72.

11 Edward M. Gramlich, "Short and Long Run Income Losses from Recession," Final Report prepared for the National Commission for Employment Policy (July 1981).

12 Louise B. Russell, *The Baby Boom Generation and the Economy* (Washington: Brookings Institution, 1982), p. 55.

13 Russell W. Rumberger, "The Changing Skill Requirements of Jobs in the U.S. Economy," *Industrial and Labor Relations Review*, Vol. 34 (July 1981), pp. 578-590.

*Chapter 3*

# Youth in Labor Market Distress

In 1980, 18 percent of teenagers were unemployed, triple the adult unemployment rate. Yet, it would be wrong to conclude that labor market distress was three times worse for teenagers than for adults. The analysis in this report indicates that for youth, as for each of the other groups under discussion, distress is highly concentrated among a relatively few members of the group[1]; it turns out to be a small problem for many and a large problem for some. To understand who in each group is likely to be in distress, it is necessary to understand the peculiarities of the labor market for each group.

Young people are typically in the process of moving from full-time student status to full-time worker status. The mix of students and workers among youth has been changing through the last few decades: in October 1950, 15 percent of youth age 18 to 24 were enrolled as students, while by 1980 that proportion had doubled.[2] As Figure 3-1 illustrates, the evolution of a cohort's work experience over time is typically a story of increasing attachment to the labor force as well as to particular firms. By age 55 to 59, almost one-third of male workers report they have been with the same firm 20 or more years.[3] Compensation also rises with experience and tenure; employers and employees become more valuable to each other as they learn about each other and adjust to make their relationship as productive as possible. Youth trying to enter the regular labor market are at the beginning of this process and hence have higher unemployment rates than they will later.

Employers seek the best available people at a given wage. For jobs where productivity depends on skills best learned at the work site, employers prefer experienced and therefore older workers, who are also more likely to have revealed some of their hidden productivity characteristics (those "fixed" factors discussed in Chapter 1). Employers are more uncertain about such characteristics in younger workers and have less evidence to offset any stereotypes they may have about a racial, ethnic or sex group's productivity. If the schools have reduced the information about the graduate that is contained in a high school diploma, the process is further complicated. Thus, employers for whom hiring costs are significant may either not hire young workers or offer them lower wages—though minimum wage laws, union contracts, corporate policy, and custom may make the latter difficult.

From a youth's point of view, there are also reasons for higher unemployment. For teenagers in school (which includes most unemployed 16 to 17 year olds), jobs have to be part-time, fit school schedules and be easy to reach with available transportation. Further, youth embarking on careers need time to find and sample jobs; over one-half of unemployed teenagers are seeking first jobs or have just reentered the labor force after doing something else. Indeed, for young people, unemployment may not even be a good term; "nonemployment" (periods for which no work is reported) and employment may be more useful categories.[4]

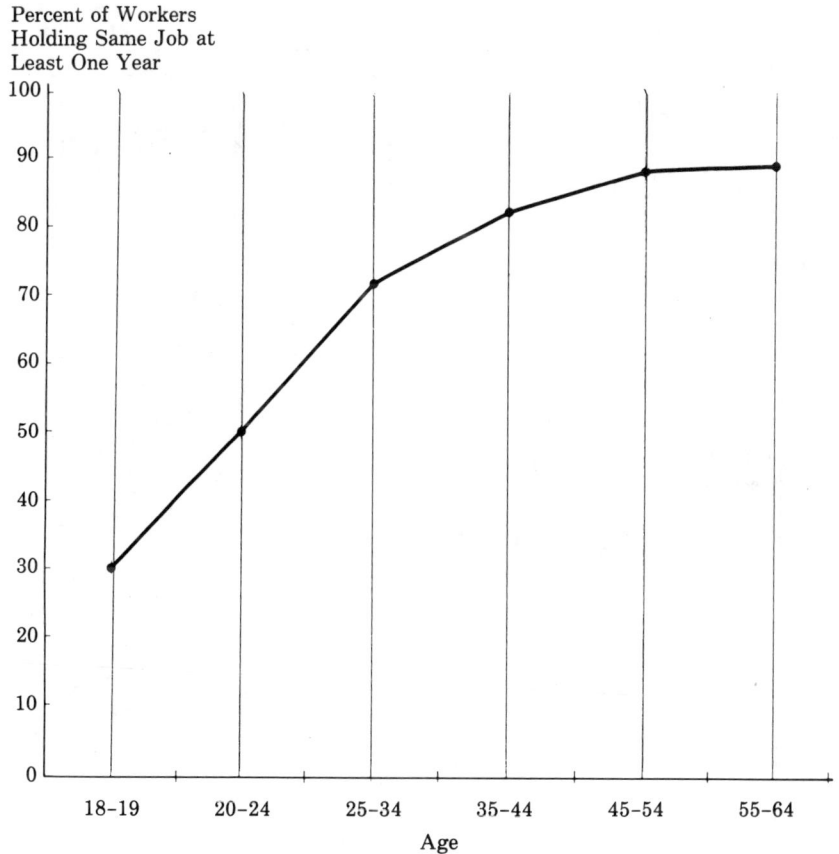

Figure 3-1. *Job Tenure of Employed Males, January 1978*

Source: Linda Leighton and Jacob Mincer, "Labor Turnover and Youth Unemployment," in Richard B. Freeman and David A. Wise, eds., *The Youth Labor Market Problem: Its Nature, Causes and Consequences* (Chicago: University of Chicago Press, 1982), p. 242.

*Figure 3-2. Unemployment Rates by Age, Sex and Race, 1969 and 1978*

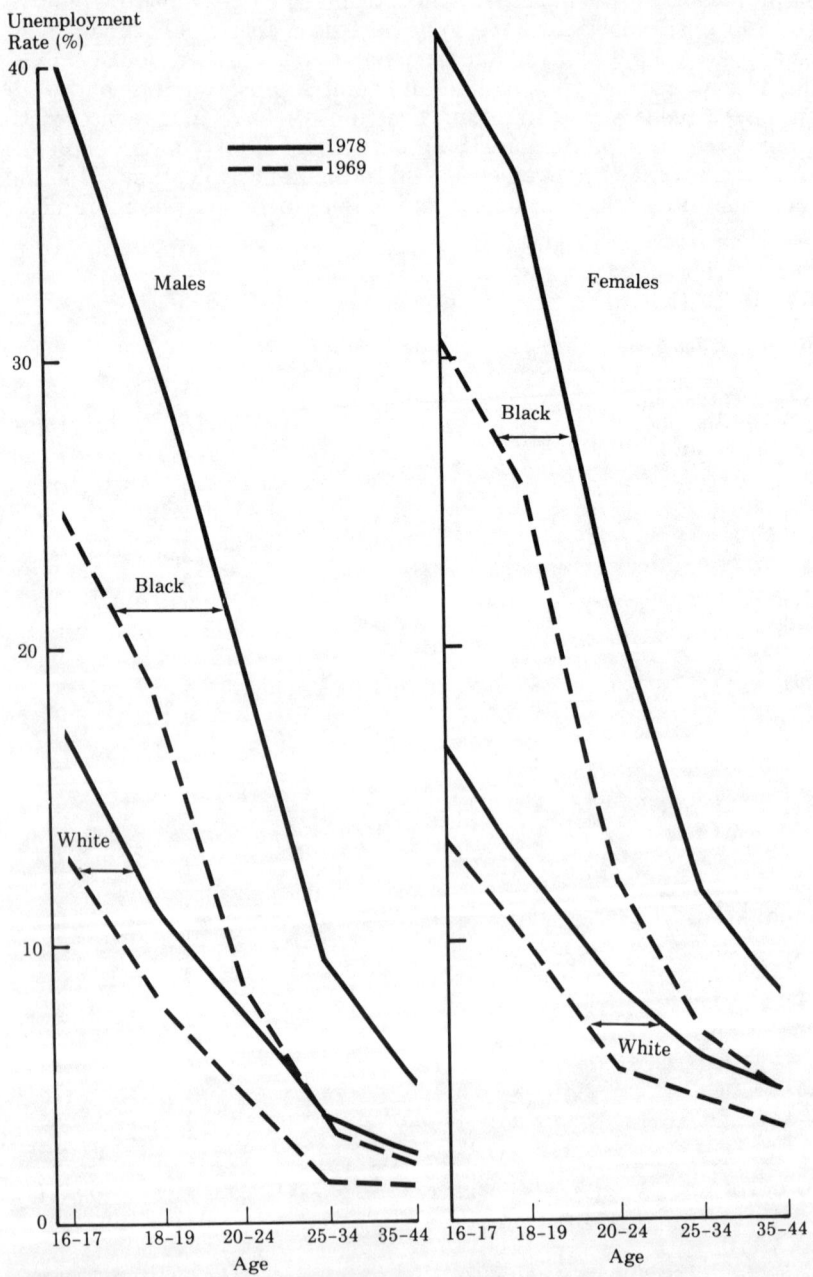

Sources: *Employment and Training Report of the President* (1978), Table A-20, and *Employment and Earnings* (January 1979), Table 3.

Figure 3-2 illustrates that the unemployment rate is typically highest for youngest workers and then falls dramatically during a cohort's first decade in the labor market. This figure also demonstrates that the age-unemployment curves shifted upward between 1969 and 1978, reflecting the maturing of the baby-boom generation and rising overall unemployment. Another dramatic aspect of Figure 3-2 is that, at all ages, the unemployment rate of blacks is at least double that of whites. How much of this is due to direct labor market discrimination against black youth and how much is due to blacks coming from poorer families, receiving worse schooling and living in areas with loose labor markets? The dimensions of labor market distress among youth in the 1980s will depend on the answers to these questions.

## The Baby Boom, the Business Cycle and Youthful Distress

Simple economic theory would predict that as the proportion of youth in the labor force increased over the 1970s, their wages would fall relative to those of other groups; only to the extent that wages were prevented by institutional and other reasons from decreasing enough to clear the youth labor market would the theory have predicted "job rationing" and higher unemployment. Russell's review of the evidence demonstrates that this simple theory does much to explain the consequences of the baby boom's maturation.[5] Figure 3-3A from Russell's review, which plots unemployment rates purged of business cycle effects by a simple statistical technique, shows no noticeable rise in the unemployment rates of young men and women during the 1970s; the rise in teenage unemployment occurred earlier, before the baby boom hit the labor market. Figure 3-3B tells the rest of the story: the wages of young people relative to those of adults have fallen consistently since 1955 and especially rapidly in the 1970s. The wages of women over age 25 seemed to hold up remarkably well, due perhaps to increasing labor market experience, new labor market opportunities and rapid growth in jobs traditionally held by women. In short, the baby boom does not seem to have been the main cause of the overall rise in youth unemployment: wages (especially for men) adjusted downward and the labor market adapted (as it does every summer) to the sudden influx of young workers.

The Russell analysis attributes most of the upward shift over the 1970s in the age-unemployment curve to business cycle conditions. Unfortunately, the maturing of the baby boom coincided with poorer economic performance, so this conclusion must be treated cautiously. However, there is no doubt that youth do relatively worse in weak labor markets. Based on data over time and across cities, the unemployment rate for youth goes up by an average of 3 to 5 percentage points when the unemployment rate for adult males rises by 1 percentage point.[6] Given this relationship, the relatively slack labor market during the 1970s can account for much of the rise in youth unemployment. The

*Figure 3-3A. Unemployment Rates Corrected for the Business Cycle, 1947-80*

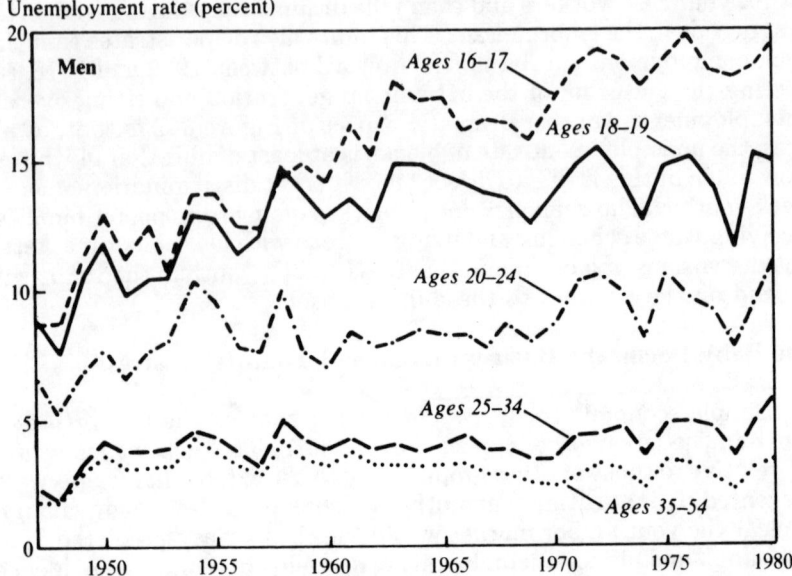

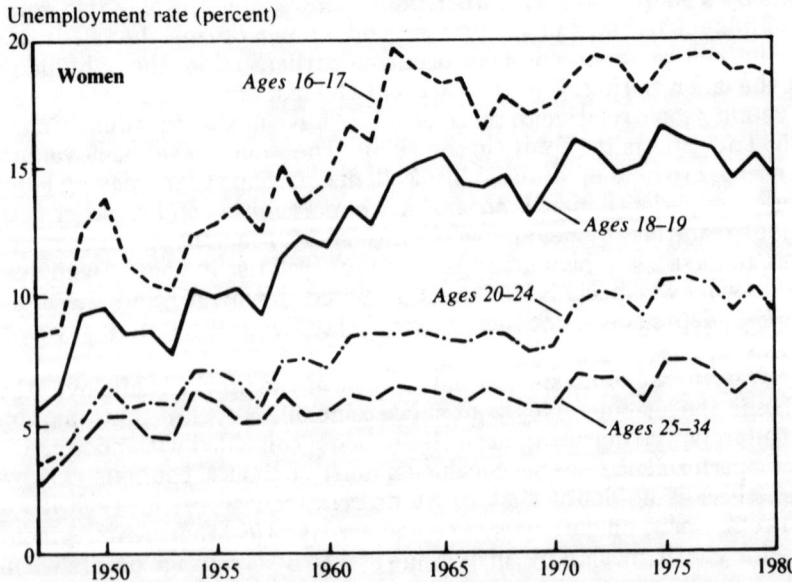

*Figure 3-3B. Ratios of Incomes of Younger Men (Women) to Those of Men (Women) Age 45 Through 54, 1955-80*

Source: Louise B. Russell, *The Baby Boom Generation and the Economy* (Washington: Brookings Institution, 1982). Reprinted with permission.

relative wages of youth declined enough to absorb the large numbers of new young workers, but the general level of real wages did not fall enough to prevent increases in overall unemployment with its usual multiplied effect on youth unemployment.

If weak labor market demand rather than the size of the baby boom cohort was responsible for most of the rise in youth unemployment rates in the 1970s, then the prospects for youth are no brighter in the 1980s. There will be fewer white youth entering the labor force (the flow of young black entrants does not start to decline until mid decade), meaning that the absolute number of unemployed youth could be smaller. But weaker demand conditions in the overall labor market will offset the reduction in cohort size, leaving youth unemployment rates about the same.

Whether youth unemployment signifies distress depends on two questions: are unemployed youth currently in distress; and does unemployment when young lead to labor market distress later in life? On the issue of current distress, it is relevant to note that, in March 1978, 81 percent of civilian black teenagers and 93 percent of civilian white teenagers age 16 to 19 were either in school, working or both, and that almost all unemployed teenage boys lived with their parents.[7] This suggests that most unemployed teenagers have productive uses for their time and reasonable living arrangements. However, living at home and going to school are the products of choices among alternatives, and youth with better job alternatives might choose differently. Furthermore, unemployment is substantially more likely for teenagers from poor families whose earnings could be the increment that raises their family out of poverty, and poor teenage students may need jobs to finance their education or support others dependent on them. Therefore, living at home or attending school does not prove that unemployment does not cause distress among youth.

The employment problems of youth are particularly important because, while a majority of teenagers have short periods of unemployment, some have long periods of looking for work and not finding it. In 1977, between 70 and 80 percent of the total number of weeks of unemployment experienced by youth was incurred by those with 15 or more weeks of unemployment. Those youth were only 8 percent of all youth in the labor force that year.[8] Table 3-1 tallies "low income" youth (those with incomes of 70 percent or less of the Bureau of Labor Statistics' lower living standard) who suffered long duration unemployment or nonemployment. Those 2.8 million youth, representing 6.5 percent of the civilian youth population in March 1978, were clearly in distress.

## The Issue of Scarring

What are the longer-term consequences of youth's lack of employment early in their careers? Some of the most interesting recent work

Table 3-1. Low Income Youth with Serious Unemployment or Nonemployment by School and Family Status, March 1978*

|  | Age 16–19 | Age 20–24 | Total |
|---|---|---|---|
|  | | (1000s) | |
| Young Men | | | |
| Students | | | |
| 1) 15+ weeks of unemployment | 57 | 12 | 69 |
| Nonstudents | | | |
| 2) 15+ weeks of unemployment | 106 | 267 | 373 |
| 3) 15+ weeks of nonemployment | 394 | 626 | 1,020 |
| Young Women | | | |
| Students | | | |
| 4) 15+ weeks of unemployment | 35 | 22 | 57 |
| Nonstudents | | | |
| Head of household with children | | | |
| 5) 15+ weeks of unemployment | 15 | 60 | 75 |
| Other family status | | | |
| 6) 15+ weeks of unemployment | 54 | 106 | 160 |
| 7) 15+ weeks of nonemployment | 420 | 646 | 1,066 |
| 1. Total, only those with substantial unemployment [1)+2)+4)+5)+6)] | 267 | 467 | 734 |
| 2. Total, expected to work with substantial nonemployment [3)+7)] | 814 | 1,272 | 2,086 |

*Youth from families with incomes below 70 percent of BLS lower living standard. Nonemployment weeks are those for which no hours of work are reported.

Source: Tabulations by Robert Lerman from *Current Population Survey* (Bureau of the Census, March 1978).

in empirical labor economics has analyzed the relationship between an individual's employment or unemployment during one period and that worker's employment and earnings later. Meyer and Wise found that persons who work while enrolled in high school tend to work more hours at higher wages in later years.[9] Lerman found that teenagers who were unemployed 15 or more weeks in one year were four times as likely as other teenagers to be unemployed in March the next year.[10] Unfortunately, these statistical correlations do not answer the question of whether unemployment is *doing* something to a person or *signaling* something about the person. It is no surprise that someone who left high school without having mastered basic skills will have lower wages and more trouble finding and keeping a first job and that these problems will persist, causing later employment difficulties. But are initial handicaps compounded by the early labor market failures themselves? Do the early labor market experiences of such young people cause their earnings to be lower throughout their lives? This possible effect is often called "scarring."

There are formidable statistical problems in sorting out how much of the persistence in low earnings or unemployment is signaling differences among workers and how much is due to injury caused by the unemployment experience. The evidence suggests that, for men, early unemployment does not (with the possible exception of inner-city black teenagers) lead to later unemployment when fixed personal and other characteristics are controlled for statistically.[11] For women, on the other hand, lack of work in one period may lower probabilities of working later, perhaps because early unemployment causes them to make decisions that reduce their commitment to or opportunities in the labor market later. It is also clear that sustained unemployment summing to at least one-half a year during the teen years will significantly lower wages as long as eight years later for *both* men and women. Ellwood also found that early work experience increased wages by as much as 10 to 20 percent a year in the first few years. He was not able to show that such differences persist, though it seems unlikely that they would as experience differences even out over a lifetime.

In short, the evidence is that long duration unemployment in the early years in the labor market will lower earnings for a long time. A cohort that has the misfortune to mature during a weak labor market will be less productive for years. Thus, youth, especially minorities, experiencing unemployment during the first part of the 1980s will have lower wages throughout the decade. For youth at greatest risk of distress, this scarring will likely offset most of the wage gains to have been expected from being in a smaller cohort.

## Structure of Labor Market Distress among Youth

There is not now nor has there been a general youth unemployment problem; rather, there is a highly concentrated problem that is worse among the poor and minorities. The problem is with the few youth suffering long duration unemployment rather than with the many youth who experience short periods of unemployment. It is particularly acute for young blacks, though the majority of distressed youth are white. While wages of employed young blacks have been converging with those of young whites, the unemployment rate differentials have widened; the employment-to-population ratio for black teenagers was not even half that of whites in 1978. The labor market problems for black youth not college bound are astonishing: in 1980, the black teen unemployment rate was 39 percent. In 1977, over one in five young black male and female members of the labor force suffered at least 15 weeks of unemployment, more than double the comparable white rate.[12]

One statistic gives a remarkable indication of the alternatives available to black youth. By conservative estimate, 42 percent of all black males born between 1957 and 1962 who were qualified for enlistment in the armed services by September 1981 had in fact chosen to enlist; this was three times the comparable military participation rate for qualified white males.[13] There is nothing wrong with young blacks choosing military service, but when young qualified black and white youth compare their opportunities in the civilian labor market with comparable military service, young black men are three times as likely to choose that military option.

The most dramatic deterioration of black relative to white teenage labor market experience can be seen in the employment-to-population ratios of the two groups. The employment rate of nonwhite male teenagers fell steadily from over 50 percent in the early 1950s to the 30 percent range in the 1970s. The comparable rate for white male teenagers, 40 percent in 1950, fell much less sharply until the mid 1960s, when it began to rise steadily, again reaching 40 percent in 1970. However, Cogan has shown that almost the entire decline between 1950 and 1970 in black teenage employment occurred because (1) black teenage employment rates in the South (where three-fourths of them lived) dropped from 55 percent in 1950 to 28 percent in 1970 as southern agriculture became less labor intensive; and (2) because black teenagers moved to other regions where their employment rates were and remained near 25 percent.[14]

The labor market performance of young blacks and other disadvantaged youth has been dismal for a variety of reasons. Cogan suggests the minimum wage may have played an important role in preventing nonagricultural employment from absorbing the young displaced blacks. There is other evidence that a 10 percent rise in the minimum wage is generally associated with a 1 to 2.5 percent decline in overall teenage employment[15] (though little evidence of effects on unemployment rates). But why are the employment prospects of disadvantaged youth particularly vulnerable to the minimum wage?

Two possible additional causes of the decline in employment rates among disadvantaged youth are rising school enrollment rates and the increasing concentration of young blacks in the central cities. By the mid 1970s, the school enrollment rates of nonwhites were at least equal to those of whites for almost every age group; as noted earlier, youth in school are less likely to be working. The other explanation heard frequently—that housing discrimination and poverty have trapped blacks in the centers of cities while jobs (and white workers) have increasingly moved to the suburbs and beyond—is not so simple.[16] As the central cities have become more black, pro-black consumer discrimination among the ghetto population could have displaced the anti-black discrimination of suburbanizing whites. In a society with discrimination, the ghetto has some potential employment benefits as well as costs, especially in the service industries and among professionals. On the other hand, for lower skilled and manufacturing jobs, increased distance and lack of public transportation to suburban jobs are likely to be more important.

Not much of the decline in employment rates among young blacks can be attributed to changes in school attendance or residential patterns. As Table 3-2 indicates, the employment rate for black males age 20-24 declined 21 percentage points from 1964 to 1978. Decomposition of that decline into changes due to redistribution of this group into different school status and residence categories versus declines within categories shows most of the decline, about 18 percentage points, was because employment rates across the board decreased dramatically from 1964 to 1978. Much the same story holds for teenage males: had there been no change in the distribution of this group among school and residence categories, the decline in employment rates in all categories would still have resulted in an 8 percentage point drop in the group employment rate from 1964 to 1978, compared to the 9 percentage point decline that actually occurred.

The employment picture for black females was almost the reverse of that for black males during the 1964-78 period. For black females age 20-24, the central cities offered the best job opportunities because the demand for clerical and service jobs traditionally performed by women has been relatively strong in central cities. For black women as well as men, the changes (increases for women, decreases for men) in employment rates within categories were much more important than

Table 3-2. *Civilian Employment-Population Ratios for Young Blacks, by Sex-Age Groups and by School and Central City Status, March 1964 and 1978*

| Sex-Age Group | Total | In School | | Not in School | |
| --- | --- | --- | --- | --- | --- |
| | | In Central City | Outside Central City | In Central City | Outside Central City |
| Males, age 16-19 | | | | | |
| 1964 | 33% | 18% | 18% | 53% | 78% |
| 1978 | 24 | 9 | 16 | 44 | 61 |
| Change, 1964-78 | −9% | −9% | −2% | −9% | −17% |
| Males, age 20-24 | | | | | |
| 1964 | 79 | 13 | 50 | 79 | 88 |
| 1978 | 58 | 7 | 5 | 65 | 69 |
| Change, 1964-78 | −21% | −6% | −45% | −14% | −19% |
| Females, age 16-19 | | | | | |
| 1964 | 16 | 8 | 7 | 28 | 30 |
| 1978 | 17 | 9 | 9 | 30 | 31 |
| Change, 1964-78 | 1% | 1% | 2% | 2% | 1% |
| Females, age 20-24 | | | | | |
| 1964 | 36 | 34 | 10 | 44 | 26 |
| 1978 | 49 | 15 | 28 | 52 | 57 |
| Change, 1964-78 | 13% | −19% | 18% | 8% | 31% |

Source: Frank Levy and Robert Lerman, "An Analysis of the Black Youth Employment Problem," in Vice President Mondale's Task Force on Youth Employment, *A Review of Youth Employment Problems, Programs and Policies*, Vol. 2 (U.S. Employment and Training Administration, Department of Labor, January 1980), pp. 6, 12.

the shifts among categories in explaining the overall change in employment rates.

In summary, the most serious question that arises from this analysis of young black employment is why, during the 1964-78 period when employment rates for most young whites were rising, did the already low employment rates of young black males decline dramatically? And, to the extent that the problem was exacerbated by the military "siphoning off" many of the most employable young black men, will planned increases in military manpower over the 1980s through explicit labor market competition (that is, without a draft) mean even further declines in black civilian employment during the decade?

Over the past decade, researchers have found many correlates of labor market distress among youth (see footnote 1). Young people of any color are more likely to have serious labor market troubles if they come from poor families, live in poverty areas, live where the mix of jobs is such that few youth are employed, and have no older employed siblings to recommend them for a job. Being black compounds all these impediments. A weak labor market and cutbacks in income transfer programs favoring families with young may increase the distress felt by youth over at least the first half of the decade.

A question raised by differential employment rates is whether the group with the lower rate may have higher reservation or target wage rates—wage rates they must be offered before they will accept a job. There is no evidence that this plays any part in the explanation of the difference between young whites and blacks. Youth often take the first job offered, and surveys have failed to find significant racial differences in reservation wages.[17] Furthermore, when poor black and white youth were guaranteed minimum wage jobs in a large government experiment during the 1970s, the employment rate for the black youth rose to that of similar whites.[18] This suggests that special efforts on the demand side of the market—to assure that jobs are available—might be effective.

Another youth group that requires special mention here is teenage mothers.[19] Women who have their first children during their teens are far more likely to cut short their education, have larger families and become locked into labor market distress. Although there is no strong evidence that the Aid to Families with Dependent Children welfare program induces higher teenage fertility, 71 percent of all AFDC mothers were teenagers when they had their first child. The good news is that the fertility rate for women age 15 to 19 has fallen steadily from its peak in 1957: for white teenagers, from 85 births per thousand women to 44.5 per thousand in 1979; for nonwhite teenagers, from 173 per thousand to 100 per thousand. The decline for both groups appears to have leveled out in the mid 1970s. Unfortunately, for black teenagers not only is the birth rate double that for whites, but 87 percent of these births are out of wedlock versus 33 percent for whites. This is a serious problem because labor market distress is far more acute for single-parent households, and out-of-wedlock births have a greater chance of generating such families.

To the extent that inadequate labor market opportunities for youth encourage teenage pregnancy, this is a very special form of the scarring discussed above. There is no persuasive evidence on this question. There is evidence that the availability of birth control methods, including abortions, has played a major role in reducing birth rates for teenage women. A 1978 study found that 38 percent of teenage pregnancies were terminated by abortion.[20] If the teenage fertility rate does not start to rise, the declining cohort of women reaching their teens will reduce the number of teenage mothers, though not, of course, their incidence. Only a further decline in their fertility will do that.

## The Role of Education

What role does education play in youth labor market distress?[21] It is known that high school dropouts and low achieving youth tend to have bad labor market experiences and that employers complain about problems with youth who cannot read well or do basic computations. In an increasingly service-oriented economy, these basic abilities are in fact important vocational skills.[22] The development of such functional literacy requires mastering earlier skills such as the simple decoding of words and phrases and simple arithmetic computations. These facts lead naturally to consideration of compensatory education policies.

One of the strongest correlates of performance by students on achievement tests is the socioeconomic status of their parents. However, evaluators have found that more school resources can improve the performance of students: more and better teachers do make a difference. Furthermore, the way in which a school's or district's resources are distributed across particular types of children will have an important effect on both the average performance of pupils and the variation in student outcomes.[23] Most of the federal compensatory education dollars under the Elementary and Secondary Education Act of 1965 have been used at elementary schools, where great gains have been made in the performance of black and disadvantaged children; by the end of the third grade, children in these programs are beginning to master the basic decoding skills in reading and simple computations.

But this encouraging finding is paired with one which suggests that the discrepancies between wealthier and poorer students at the junior and senior high school level are not being rapidly eliminated.[24] The simple story seems to be that poor children are taught how to sound out words but not the higher-order skills in word use necessary for functional literacy and for successful economic performance later in life. The junior and senior high schools in this country are not performing well, and federal aid has had relatively little impact at those levels.

The Vocational Education Act is the other major federal program that helps fund mainline state and local educational institutions. Most of this money ends up as basic grants for secondary vocational education and generally provides less than 10 percent of the state and local expenditures on such education. This is not a compensatory program; the objective is mainly to improve the vocational skills of the overall population.

While vocational education is expensive, evaluations show it is not associated with higher subsequent earnings for its male students,[25] except for gains lasting less than five years for those in industrial arts curricula. Female students tend to get shunted into traditionally "female" clerical occupations via this system and to have higher earnings for the first five years of their careers than women who do not get such training. Vocational education also seems to have little effect on the dropout behavior of students.

In summary, the vocational education system appears to produce only short-term earnings gains. These findings are disturbing because it would seem self-evident that training high school students for jobs should improve their experiences in the labor market. Of course, some high quality vocational high schools do pay off handsomely for those lucky enough to attend. The fundamental issue is whether schools should concentrate on giving students basic functional skills (that could include basic manual skills) or should help them learn specific occupational skills. Some skills, such as typing, seem to be taught well in a classroom setting, but other skills do not. Even when they are, the training often becomes obsolete rapidly if the industry undergoes technological change.

The most serious education problem affecting youth labor market performance is that so many students drop out of high school. The dropout rate in cities such as New York has approached 45 percent. The Federal Youth Entitlement Demonstration Program was designed to test whether offering high school students part-time jobs during the school year and full-time summer jobs would induce them to stay in school or, for dropouts, get them back into school. One of the most crucial aspects of the program was the establishment of alternative schools for those who wanted them. The program seems to have had little impact on dropout rates; but it did get dropouts back into alternative schools and (especially for blacks) increase their in-school employment. Because of the design of the experiment, it is not known whether it was the alternative school or the job or both that got dropouts back.[26]

## Conclusion

This discussion of youth has been extensive because it is when a cohort first enters the labor market that its members who are likely to be in permanent distress are first revealed. Since only a few million people are involved, it is tempting to say that there must be an easy solution to their problems. But the problems have to do with the poverty of parents, discrimination and the inability of the educational system to change what society "hath wrought." Some programs that might be considered could create adverse incentives and even delay adjustment. There are examples of effective programs, such as the Job Corps that takes youth with little prospect of success, removes them from their normal environment and provides intensive and expensive (almost $8,000 per participant) remedial efforts. The rate of return on a Job Corps investment is fairly high and so is the dropout rate.

The problem for policy is rather difficult. In the interests of maintaining social and economic mobility, youth are not put in rigid tracks and are not often provided with the special intensive schooling that might be especially beneficial to those likely to be in distress later. The market is relied upon to sort these new workers into the "right" jobs and to provide the training they need. Special school-to-work transition programs can speed the process, but their gains are short lived, and so they make sense only if inexpensive. By and large, the system works fairly well. But for some 10 percent of the population, the system works hardly at all; for them, labor market distress is formidable and long lived. It is particularly acute for poor blacks, and there is no reason to expect a substantial change in the nature or site of the problem during the 1980s.

## Notes

1 Fortunately, a great deal more is now known about the nature of youth labor market problems because of several impressive bodies of research done during the past few years. The most important of these is contained in Richard B. Freeman and David A. Wise, eds., *The Youth Labor Market Problem: Its Nature, Causes, and Consequences* (Chicago: University of Chicago Press, 1982), p. 555. Two other especially useful documents are Paul Osterman's book, *Getting Started: the Youth Labor Market* (Cambridge, Mass.: MIT Press, 1980), p. 197, and some of the papers in the research volumes published by Vice President Mondale's Task Force on Youth Employment, *The Youth Employment Problem: Causes and Dimensions*, Vols. 1–3 (1980). Some of what follows draws on a previous literature review by Daniel H. Saks and Ralph E. Smith, "Youth with poor job prospects," *Education and Urban Society*, Vol. 14, No. 1 (November 1981), pp. 15–32.

2 Cited in Louise B. Russell, *The Baby Boom Generation and the Economy* (Washington: Brookings Institution, 1982), p. 23.

3 Calculated from data in Bureau of Labor Statistics, *Tenure of Current Job by Sex, January 1978*, Special Labor Force Report 235 (BLS, 1979).

4 See Kim B. Clark and Lawrence H. Summers, "The Dynamics of Youth Unemployment," in Freeman and Wise, *The Youth Labor Market Problem*.

5 Russell, *The Baby Boom Generation*, pp. 60, 73, 77. Michael Wachter and Choongsoo Kim, "Time Series Changes in Youth Joblessness," in Freeman and Wise, *The Youth Labor Market Problem*, take a similar perspective, though they assign much more of an effect to the large baby-boom cohort causing the higher unemployment (especially for teenagers) and much less labor force participation for blacks. It is the confusion between the baby boom and a simple time trend that makes it hard to be extremely confident about any conclusions.

## Notes

6 Freeman and Wise, *The Youth Labor Market Problem*, p. 10.

7 Martin Feldstein and David T. Ellwood, "Teenage Unemployment: What Is the Problem?", in Freeman and Wise, *The Youth Labor Market Problem*, p. 19.

8 Robert Lerman, "An Analysis of Youth Employment Problems," in Task Force on Youth Employment, *A Review of Youth Employment*, Vol. 1 (January 1980).

9 Robert H. Meyer and David A. Wise, "High School Preparation and Early Labor Force Experience," in Freeman and Wise, *The Youth Labor Market Problem*, pp. 277–348.

10 Robert Lerman et al., *Concepts and Measures of Structural Unemployment* (Department of Labor, 1979).

11 See David T. Ellwood, "Teenage Unemployment: Permanent Scars or Temporary Blemishes?", Mary Corcoran, "The Employment and Wage Consequences of Teenage Women's Nonemployment," and Meyer and Wise, "High School Preparation," all in Freeman and Wise, *The Youth Labor Market Problem*.

12 Lerman, "An Analysis of Youth Employment Problems."

13 Martin Binkin and Mary J. Eitelberg et al., *Blacks and the Military* (Washington: Brookings Institution, 1982), p. 66. The differential quality of environment and schooling across the two groups is indicated by the fact that only 44 percent of the blacks in that birth cohort, compared with 85 percent of whites, would have qualified for military service.

14 John Cogan, "The Decline in Black Teenage Employment: 1950–70," *American Economic Review*, Vol. 72 (September 1982), pp. 621–638.

15 Minimum Wage Study Commission, *Report*, Vol. 1 (May 1981), pp. 31–61.

16 Paul Offner and Daniel H. Saks, "A Note on John Kain's 'Housing Segregation, Negro Employment and Metropolitan Decentralization,'" *Quarterly Journal of Economics*, Vol. 85, No. 1 (February 1971), pp. 147–160.

17 Paul Osterman, "The Employment Problems of Black Youth: A Review of the Evidence and Some Policy Suggestions," in Task Force on Youth Employment, *A Review of Youth Employment Problems*, Vol. 2 (1980).

18 George Farkas et al., *Early Impacts from the Youth Entitlement Demonstration: Participation, Work, and Schooling* (Manpower Demonstration Research Corp., 1980).

19 An excellent review of these issues is in Kristin A. Moore and Martha R. Burt, *Private Crisis, Public Costs* (Washington: Urban Institute Press, 1982), p. 166.

20 As reported in ibid., p. 82.

21 This section is mostly taken from Saks and Smith, "Youth with poor job prospects," pp. 26–28.

22 The question of industrial mix and the changing demand for skills will be addressed in Chapter 5, "Dislocated Workers."

23 For a review, see Byron Brown and Daniel H. Saks, "The Microeconomics of Schooling," *Review of Research in Education*, Vol. 9 (1981), pp. 217–256.

24 National Assessment of Educational Progress, *Three National Assessments of Reading: Changes in Performance, 1970-80,* Report No. 11-R-01 (April 1981).

25 The best work on this subject was done for the National Commission for Employment Policy by Robert H. Meyer and is discussed in *The Federal Role in Vocational Education,* Report No. 12 (September 1981), pp. 10-39. To an economist, this finding should not be surprising. If each student is trying to select the curriculum that will result in the highest subsequent earnings and there are no entry restrictions, then at the margin the private rate of return will be the same in each curriculum. Since the cost to the student is the same, equal rates of return are obtained by having equal benefits. The point is that the subsidy has caused overproduction and the policy question is whether that is desirable.

26 Farkas et al., *Early Impacts.*

## Chapter 4
# Disadvantaged Adults

Do many members of a cohort tend to have inadequate earnings during their prime ages? What are the characteristics of these low earners? Are there particular groups with a high incidence of persistent distress? The next chapter will focus on those whose earnings suddenly collapse; here, persistent poor earnings among prime-age workers are examined.

This chapter provides an elaboration of the concepts introduced in Chapter 1 concerning earnings variability and the concentrated nature of long duration unemployment. The analysis examines first the stability over time of the earnings distribution and then the stability of the position of individuals and families within that distribution. Some of the factors associated with persistent low earnings and the special characteristics of particular low earning groups are discussed.

Table 4-1 shows the share of total U.S. income going to each one-fifth of the families in America, ordered from lowest to highest income. The Total Cash Income column includes income from government transfer programs, while the Pretransfer Income column nets out such income (though it does not attempt to adjust for changes in behavior that might be induced were those transfers actually unavailable). The distribution of pretransfer income became more unequal between 1965 and 1978; only when transfers are included does the distribution of cash income stay relatively stable.

The increased inequality of pretransfer family income is largely the result of the changed distribution of family types. Compared to 1965, in 1978 there were more two-earner upper middle-class families, young

Table 4-1. *Distribution of Income for Families and Unrelated Individuals, 1965 and 1978*

| | Percent of Total Income Received by Each Quintile | | | |
|---|---|---|---|---|
| | 1965 | | 1978 | |
| Quintile | Pretransfer Income | Total Cash Income | Pretransfer Income | Total Cash Income |
| 1 | 1.32 | 3.93 | 0.76 | 3.86 |
| 2 | 9.62 | 10.82 | 7.77 | 9.85 |
| 3 | 17.99 | 17.65 | 16.82 | 16.74 |
| 4 | 26.05 | 24.97 | 26.69 | 25.17 |
| 5 | 45.03 | 42.62 | 47.95 | 44.38 |

Source: Computations by Institute for Research on Poverty "A Grant Application Submitted to the Assistant Secretary for Policy Evaluation at the Department of Health and Human Services" (Madison, Wis.: University of Wisconsin, February 1981), p. 8.

families with low earnings and poor older families receiving transfers. The distribution of earnings within groups of similar families appears to have remained remarkably stable during this period. For example, the distribution of the earnings of full-time male workers changed very little.[1]

Another way of seeing this stability is to look at the poverty rate. Over the 1970s, the pretransfer poverty rate was fairly stable at around 20 percent of families. Some 40 percent of those pretransfer poor were lifted out of poverty by cash transfer programs and perhaps an additional 25 percent by in-kind transfers, leaving about a third of the pretransfer families (about 6 percent of all families) in poverty in 1979.[2] This overall effect of the transfer program cloaks considerable variation among groups, with cash transfers to older households eliminating over 70 percent of those poor in 1978 (compared to 50 percent in 1965) but only about 20 percent of the fastest rising poverty group, households headed by working-age women.[3]

Since the distribution of earnings was stable and the improvements in poverty over the decade were accomplished through transfers, are those workers at the lower end of that earnings distribution in any year likely to remain there? The discussion of earnings mobility in Chapter 1 dealt with the entire distribution; under discussion here are only those at the bottom of the distribution.

Freeman examined data from a national survey that followed the same households for the 10 years 1969 to 1978.[4] He counted, for each household, the number of years in which the male head had earnings in the lowest decile of full-time male earnings for that year (for example, annual earnings below $7,236 in 1978). As Figure 4-1 shows, in the 1969-78 period, 70.5 percent of the adult male household heads regularly in the labor force never had annual earnings in the lowest decile, while 11.1 percent had annual earnings that low exactly 1 of the 10 years, and 1.6 percent were in the lowest decile every year of the 10.

One in 20 of the males in the sample $(1.1 + 1.2 + 1.3 + 1.6 = 5.2$ percent) were in the lowest decile at least 7 of the 10 years. This group can be thought of as the hard core disadvantaged who are regularly unable to earn enough, even though they are always in the labor force. For every one of these hard core, there are almost 5 others (24.3 percent) in the lowest decile in at least 1 of the 10 years. The hard core group accounted for 44 percent of all the person years ever observed in the lowest decile. Thus, a substantial part of the sample (almost one-third) experienced low earnings for at least a temporary period, yet almost half the low earnings were of long duration. It is the same type of result as that cited earlier for unemployment: a few with long durations and many with short durations.

Table 4-2 displays the results for women in the sample who headed households over the entire decade of study. Of these women in the labor force in all 10 years, 20.7 percent had earnings in the lowest decile of the male earnings distribution every single year. This is 13 times the comparable figure (1.6 percent) for males and reflects mainly the lower earnings of working women compared to those of men. About half the women who were in the labor force 8 or 9 of the 10 years had earnings in the lowest male decile every year. For the entire sample of women, their earnings were in the lowest male decile 39.3 percent of all years and 60.2 percent of their total years in the labor force.

Figure 4-1. *Distribution of the Number of Years (of 10) in which a Male Household Head Had Annual Earnings in the Lowest Decile of Income Distribution for that Year, 1969-78*

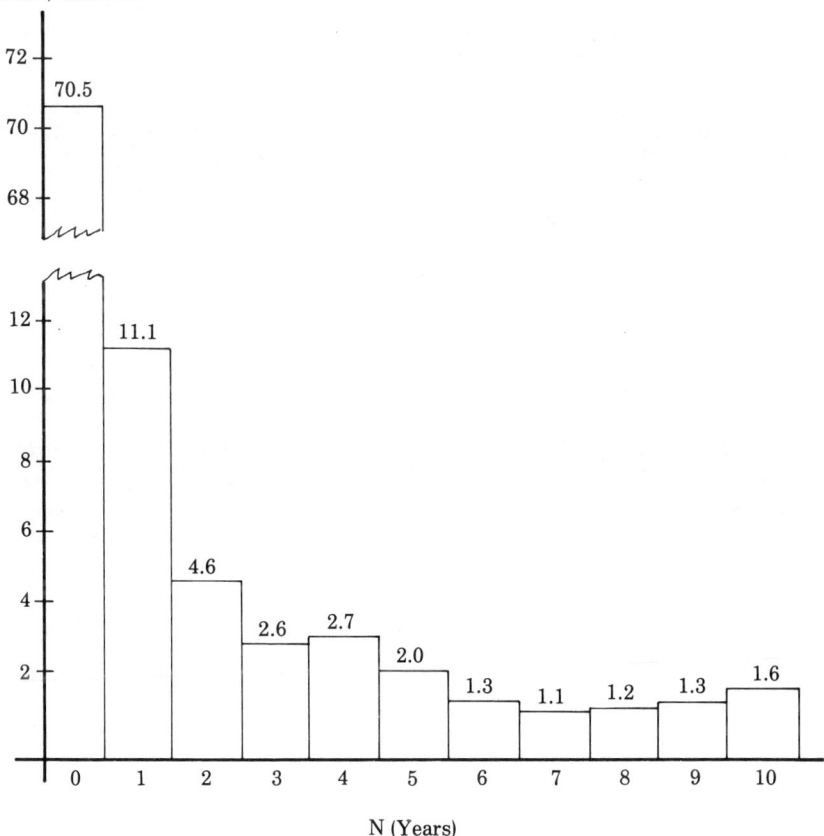

Source: Author's calculations from Richard B. Freeman in *The Federal Interest in Employment and Training* (National Commission for Employment Policy, October 1981), p. 112.

Table 4-2. Labor Market Performance of Female Household Heads,* 1969-78

| Number of Years in Labor Force, of the 10 years, 1969-78 | Percent of Sample in Group | Percent of Years in Labor Force in which Annual Earnings Were in Bottom Male Decile | Percent of Group with Annual Earnings in Bottom Male Decile, in Every Year in Labor Force |
|---|---|---|---|
| 0 | 34.8 | — | — |
| 1 | 4.4 | 92.3 | 92.3 |
| 2 | 3.6 | 91.4 | 82.7 |
| 3 | 1.9 | 82.1 | 80.2 |
| 4 | 2.7 | 66.9 | 42.0 |
| 5 | 3.9 | 54.3 | 44.5 |
| 6 | 2.5 | 96.4 | 79.7 |
| 7 | 5.4 | 67.1 | 39.3 |
| 8 | 6.2 | 75.0 | 55.6 |
| 9 | 6.6 | 60.5 | 41.6 |
| 10 | 28.1 | 42.0 | 20.7 |

Average years in labor force = 7.5 years
Percentage of total years in lowest decile = 39.3%
Percentage of total years in labor force in lowest decile = 60.2%

*All figures were based on weighted observations. The sample was limited to women who were household heads over the entire 10-year period; 80.8 percent of women who were heads in the initial year (1969) were heads for all the years, whereas 19.2 percent were not heads for all 10 years.

Source: Freeman, *The Federal Interest.*

The hard core of disadvantaged adults can be defined as those household heads regularly in the labor market whose annual earnings are in the lowest decile of the male earnings distribution every year (for women) or at least 70 percent of the years (for men). For the sample and the years used by Freeman, this definition includes 5.2 percent of men and 20.7 percent of women, or a total of about 5 million households. This is, however, a highly restrictive definition: the number of males included can be increased by almost two-thirds simply by counting those in the lowest decile at least half the time.

It also must be noted that, in the Freeman sample, the average male head provided only 54 percent of his family's income; his wife earned 16 percent. Still, the average family headed by a male whose earnings were in the lowest decile 70 percent of the time was very close to poverty. That disadvantaged male head typically did not have low earnings because he worked fewer hours; his annual hours of work were only a few percentage points lower than those of the average male worker. Rather, the problem was that his hourly wage was only $2.31 compared to the $6.80 average.

As discussed in Chapter 1, labor economists have found that much of the variation in regular wages can be "explained" by education, race, sex, lack of work experience, and industry of employment. These variables also indicate the probability that a worker will be among the disadvantaged. However, Freeman found that the best single way to predict whether someone is going to be earnings poor this year is *not* to know whether he is black, uneducated or with any other typically measured attribute, but rather to know if he was earnings poor *last* year. This corroborates the results of studies discussed in Chapter 1: fixed unmeasured characteristics are an important cause of low earnings.

A few measured attributes likely to be associated with being a disadvantaged adult are discussed briefly: being black, Hispanic and a female head of household.

## Disadvantaged Blacks—The Problem of Bifurcation

For most immigrant groups, the process of acculturation and economic progress has taken only about a generation. Blacks have been the singular exception. However, the earnings story over the past decade or so suggests that, after generations, some progress is being made against the most persistent and pernicious problem of discrimination in society.

Table 4-3, compiled by Freeman, tells the story well. In 1949, the greatest degree of earnings discrimination was against the most educated blacks. Black male college graduates in their late twenties earned only two-thirds as much as their white counterparts, while black male high school graduates earned almost three-fourths as much as their white counterparts. Part of these differences was due to the systematic discrimination within the education system that consistently directed fewer resources toward black children, and part was discrimination in the job market. By the late 1970s, young black college graduates had achieved parity with their white counterparts. Further, black workers had substantially progressed into craft and upper level management occupations. With these types of gains solidified, the prospects for blacks in the 1980s appear to be much improved. Blacks in management positions should make it difficult to engage in systematic racial discrimination at many work places—although it should be kept in mind that in 1979 a black was overall only 37 percent as likely as a white to be a manager.

However, researchers are beginning to discover that a major bifurcation is occurring in the black labor market: the well educated are doing relatively well and *average* black earnings are going up; but the average is increasing in part because many of the lowest earning blacks are not spending as much time in the labor force or at work and hence are not weighted as heavily in the earnings statistics. It appears that wage discrimination is being replaced by "quality" discrimination, a phenomenon that Pascal and Rapping noted in major league baseball in the 1970s.[5] They found that black baseball players received the same pay as white players of equal measured ability, but that black players had to meet a higher quality standard before being sent up from the

*Table 4-3. Evidence of Economic Changes for Black Americans, 1949-79*
(Black/White Ratio)

| Males | | | | | |
|---|---|---|---|---|---|
| 1. *Median wages and salaries*[1] | 1949 | 1964 | 1969 | 1979 | Change, 1969-79 |
| All workers, year- | .50 | .59 | .67 | .72 | .05 |
| round and full-time | .64 (1955) | .66 | .69 | .76 | .07 |
| 2. *Median usual weekly earnings*[2] | — | .69 (1967) | .71 | .78 (1978) | .07 |
| 3. *Median income or mean earnings by age, year-round full-time workers*[3] | 1949 | 1959 | 1969 | 1979 | Change, 1969-79 |
| 20-24 | .66 | .64 | .82 | .77 | -.05 |
| 25-34 | .60 | .61 | .72 | .74 | .02 |
| 35-44 | .55 | .59 | .68 | .78 | .10 |
| 45-54 | .54 | .55 | .68 | .59 | -.09 |
| 4. *Median income or mean earnings for young men age 25-29, by education*[3] | 1949 | 1959 | 1969 | 1978 | Change, 1969-78 |
| High school graduates | .73 | .70 | .77 | .81 | .04 |
| College graduates | .67 | .70 | .83 | 1.06 | .23 |
| 5. *Ratio of percent of all nonwhites employed in occupations to percent of all whites in occupations (age 15+)* | 1950 | 1964 | 1969 | 1979 | Change, 1969-79 |
| Professionals | .39 | .45 | .48 | .54 | .06 |
| Managers | .22 | .22 | .28 | .37 | .09 |
| Craftspeople | .41 | .58 | .68 | .81 | .13 |
| Managers, college graduates only | .42 | .41 | .49 | .75 | .26 |
| 6. *Ratio of employment to population*[4] | 1950 | 1964 | 1969 | 1979 | Change, 1950-79 |
| Black | .76 | .73 | .73 | .64 | -.12 |
| White | .81 (1954) | .78 | .78 | .75 | -.06 |
| 7. *Labor force participation rates (percent)* | | | | | |
| Black | 85.2 | 80.0 | 76.9 | 71.9 | -13.3 |
| White | 85.6 (1954) | 81.1 | 80.2 | 78.6 | - 7.0 |
| 8. *Proportion age 14+ without labor market earnings*[5] | | | | | Change, 1969-79 |
| Black | — | — | .19 | .29 | .10 |
| White | — | — | .12 | .15 (1978) | .03 |

1 Ratio of blacks' and other races' earnings to whites.
2 May *Current Population Survey*.
3 Ratio of blacks to all other workers.
4 Calculated as the (labor participation rate)/(1-unemployment rate).
5 Calculated as (all persons-number with wage or salary income, farm income or self-employment nonfarm income)/all persons.
Source: Freeman, *The Federal Interest*.

minor leagues. This is a way that prejudice can be acted on when wage discrimination is awkward.

This selection phenomenon may be occurring more widely, with government transfer programs cushioning the impact.[6] In 1968, the earnings of the average black prime-age (20-55), full-time, full-year male *worker* was 66 percent of the earnings of his white counterpart; by 1978, that ratio had risen to 76 percent. But the median earnings of *all* prime-age male blacks (counting those outside as well as in the labor force) fell over the same period from 64 to 59 percent of those of their white counterparts. The ratio of full-time, full-year black male workers to all black males in the prime-age group decreased during the period from 65 to 56 percent, while for whites the drop was only from 74 to 70 percent. Finally, the proportion of black males with no wage and salary income had grown to 11 percent by the late 1970s compared with 6 percent in 1968 and compared with 4 percent for whites in 1978. This is disturbing evidence that some of the economy-wide improvement in reported black relative earnings is the result of pruning the lowest wage blacks from the labor force. Whether the genuine advances of young well-educated blacks is the more important phenomenon and the selection problem just a transitory adjustment remains to be seen.

## Hispanics—Education and Acculturation

Depending on assumptions about the rate of immigration, the U.S. Hispanic population could grow by 2 to 4 percent per year over the next decade; the Hispanic labor force could be from 6 to 10 percent of the labor force by 1995.[7] In 1975, the median wage and salary income of Hispanic families was even lower than that of black families—only 71 percent of white Anglo family income. However, there are differences among Hispanic groups even after controlling for different measured qualifications: Cubans earn the most, followed by Mexicans, then Puerto Ricans, then others from Central and South America.

A recent study by Gould, McMannus and Welch tried to determine whether the low earnings of Hispanics are due to characteristics of the Hispanic population that might change over time.[8] Using data collected in 1976, they found that Hispanic labor market experiences in the United States were comparable to those of most other immigrant groups. Immigrants who stay long enough eventually earn more than comparable native born Americans, in large part because of migrants' self-selection for traits that the labor market values (see Chapter 1). They found that the earnings of native-born Hispanics with no English language difficulty were the same as those of Anglos with the same levels of school attainment, work experience and region of residence, and that differences in earnings could be explained in terms of these variables.

Care must be taken in drawing inferences from such a result. English language difficulty appears in this analysis to be a proxy for the degree of assimilation rather than a measure of the degree to which poor English actually interferes with productive economic activity. The study found the same effect where there were concentrations of Hispanic residents, despite expectations that speaking Spanish in such locations would have advantages. Thus, the finding is really that once language assimilation occurs and education attainment is equalized, earnings also equalize. But this can take a long time, and the process of transition can be difficult and require considerable aid. If schools do not effectively educate Hispanic children, it will be a long time before school attainment improves and earnings potentials equalize.

Depending on decisions about immigration (see the discussion in Chapter 2), Hispanics in serious labor market difficulty are likely to become more numerous over the decade. The good news is that acculturation and education may remove systematic earnings differentials. The policy issue is how best to do this. Given the nation's experience with these issues, the process need not be particularly prolonged or painful.

**Female-headed Families**

The most rapidly growing group in labor market distress over recent decades consists of households headed by females.[9] In 1970, such households were 11 percent of all families; by 1978, they were 14 percent. Among blacks, half the children are living in female-headed homes, which constitute 40 percent of black households. Because female heads of household do not, on average, work as many hours or have wage rates as high as their male counterparts, their households have significantly lower incomes, on average, as illustrated by the following comparisons: the median income of female-headed households where the woman is a full-time, full-year worker was only 59 percent of the income of similar male-headed households; the average female-headed household had only 44 percent of the median income of households with a male head; the poverty rate among female-headed households was 31 percent in 1978, six times that of households with a male head. Furthermore, while two-thirds of the income of all female-headed households is derived from labor market earnings, only one-third of the income of *poor* female-headed households is earned. In 1979, two-thirds of all female heads of household with children were in the labor force. This 10 percent increase over the 1970s was caused by increased work incentives in the welfare system[10] and the increased labor force participation of women generally.

As noted above, the low earnings of women tend to persist from year to year. Since there has been little change in the female-to-male wage ratio over the past decades, there is little reason to expect any improvement in the situation for this group. Indeed, the only substantial source of improvement in family income for female-headed households usually occurs for those who marry. Three-fourths of women who divorce before age 30 remarry within three years. However, it is also true that in Freeman's sample of all female-headed households in 1969, 80 percent maintained that status throughout the decade they were followed.

This growing group faces great labor market distress. Further, recent changes in welfare laws have reduced the incentive for many of these women to work. The CETA program appears to have been successful in training such women,[11] suggesting that there may be substantial gains for this group if the right policies are pursued.

## Conclusion

Analysis of data from the 1970s has identified a relatively small group in serious and persistent labor market distress. As youth, many of these people were often in serious labor market difficulty and, as Chapter 6 shows, many will face premature retirement and perhaps early death. This hard core group is likely to be at least as large over the 1980s as it was in the 1970s because of a weakened labor market and various trends that do not offer much hope of substantial improvement in their situation.

## Notes

1 Calculated by Richard B. Freeman in an excellent report to the National Commission for Employment Policy that has heavily influenced what is written here. See "Appendix A, Troubled Workers in the Labor Market" in the Commission's Seventh Annual Report, *The Federal Interest in Employment and Training* (October 1981), pp. 103-174.

2 According to Sheldon Danziger, the poverty population may have risen by one-third in 1981 and more in 1982. For a more detailed discussion of recent developments, see Joel Havemann et al., "Sharing the Wealth," *National Journal,* Vol. 14, No. 43 (October 13, 1982), pp. 1788-1800.

3 Institute for Research on Poverty, "A Grant Application Submitted to the Assistant Secretary for Policy Evaluation at the Department of Health and Human Services" (Madison, Wis.: University of Wisconsin, February 1981), p. 14.

4 Freeman, *The Federal Interest.*

5 This was pointed out by Frank Levy, "Changes in Employment Prospects for Black Males," *Brookings Papers on Economic Activity,* Vol. 2 (1980), pp. 513-538. See Anthony H. Pascal and Leonard A. Rapping, "The Economics of Discrimination in Organized Baseball," in Anthony H. Pascal, ed., *Racial Discrimination in Economic Life* (Lexington Books, 1972), pp. 119-156.

6 The following discussion is based on data in Levy, "Changes in Employment Prospects." The point about the economy-wide selection problem was given prominence by Richard Butler and James J. Heckman, "The Impact of the Government on the Labor Market Status of Black Americans: A Critical Review of the Literature and New Evidence," in Leonard S. Hausman et al., eds., *Equal Rights and Industrial Relations* (Madison, Wis.:

Industrial Relations Research Association, 1977). Another paper reinforcing these findings is William A. Darity, Jr. and Samuel L. Myers, Jr., "Black Economic Progress: A Case Against the Dramatic Improvement Hypothesis" (Madison, Wis.: Institute for Research on Poverty, Discussion Paper 613-80, May 1980).

7 Douglas S. Massey, "Patterns and Effects of Hispanic Immigration to the United States" (unpublished report to the National Commission for Employment Policy, March 1982).

8 William Gould, Walter McMannus and Finis Welch, "Hispanic Earnings Differentials: The Role of English Language Proficiency" (unpublished report to the National Commission for Employment Policy, by Unicon, March 1982).

9 Much of the following is from Freeman, *The Federal Interest*.

10 For more detailed discussion, see Daniel H. Saks, *Public Assistance for Mothers in an Urban Labor Market* (Princeton University, Industrial Relations Section, 1975).

11 National Commission for Employment Policy, *CETA Training Programs: Do They Work for Adults* (July 1982).

Chapter 5
# Dislocated Workers

Dislocated workers are experienced workers settled into reasonably good and sometimes excellent jobs who are suddenly confronted with the prospect of long duration unemployment and loss of earnings because, for example, their job has been eliminated or their employer has closed the plant. While most laid-off workers are eventually recalled or are able to find other jobs—if not immediately, then when the economy picks up—there are many others who are not. This chapter examines who among these dislocated workers is in distress and why, and then discusses whether changes in the economy over the 1980s are likely to increase that distress.

As with other groups discussed in this report, only a minority of dislocated workers will be shown to be in distress. By definition, distress will be concentrated in industries and regions undergoing secular and structural decline, not just cyclical fluctuations. The problem with writing about dislocation during a severe recession is that there are confusing signals about cyclical versus structural changes in employment. The economist tends to assume that the cycle will turn up again; others may not be as sure. But if high unemployment lasts long enough, the cyclically unemployed can become the structurally unemployed.

Another problem in writing about dislocation is that even the sophisticated analyst may misinterpret certain events. Norbert Wiener was a great genius, but his prediction that automation would create vast unemployment during the 1970s was not born out. The economy is so big and varied that it is not easily derailed, even by major innovations. Fundamental changes can occur, as they have in the past, without causing widespread distress. Innovations such as automation and robotics will transform the scope and nature of manufacturing employment, just as the mechanization of agriculture resulted in far-reaching and dramatic changes (including a large decrease in numbers) in agricultural employment. But in a dynamic and flexible economy, there is likely to be ample opportunity to make these changes through attrition and evolutionary adjustment.[1]

Furthermore, indirect as well as direct dislocations stemming from an innovation need to be considered. Computer aided design and manufacturing and the general application of microchips can be expected to change the entire nature and organization of work, and not just in electronics and manufacturing. After all, the impact of the automobile was hardly confined to the displacement of the horse and buggy; the structure of our cities and culture was profoundly affected, and entire new industries were created. But those adjustments took at least half a century.

This is not to say that the changes caused by modern information transfer and processing technology will be less consequential than those wrought by the automobile. Rather, the argument is that these changes also will be profound, unpredictable, job-creating as well as job-displacing, and a long time in working themselves through the system. The adjustments will cause problems similar in kind and degree to those continually dealt with in a dynamic economy; they should be manageable with limited distress unless required adjustments are impeded so that large segments of the economy become uncompetitive.

Adjustment and compensation are at the core of the dislocated worker problem. A healthy economy is constantly undergoing adjustments that are costly to some people and beneficial to others. Workers in declining industries, firms, occupations, and regions bear much of the burden of the adjustment process and have every incentive to resist it. It is especially important to aid their adjustment and for the winners to share some of the gains with the losers; otherwise, the costs and benefits of change will be unfairly distributed, physical and human resources may not be reallocated to more productive uses, and the potential output of the economy will decline.

The fundamental point is that a dynamic economy is always creating dislocations; whether the immediate cause is international trade, technological change or something else is not the real issue. The questions are: who of those dislocated by change are actually in distress; under what circumstances should they be helped to readjust; under what circumstances should they be compensated and to what extent; and under what circumstances should they be left to fend for themselves on the grounds that society cannot and should not compensate everyone for losses that are, at least in some cases, the result of individual choices.

For the purposes of this study, the need for and consequences of compensation are not at issue. Instead, two questions will be addressed: when is a dislocated worker in distress; and what industrial, occupational and regional developments are expected in the 1980s that will affect the extent and severity of dislocation?

## Dislocation and Distress

Chapter 1 reported that for male heads of household, whether or not poor, 60 percent of any random earnings dislocation faded away each year. However, for discussions of distress, it is important to know how dislocations affect low income people in particular. Accordingly, Bloom calculated the fade-out rate for earnings dislocations among CETA eligibles (low income or unemployed people) in the mid 1970s.[2] He found that, on average, 67 percent of any earnings dislocation for males and 48 percent for females faded away each year. This means that, on average, it takes four years for a man's earnings dislocation to fade to 1 percent of its starting value but seven years for a woman's, which suggests that the dislocation problem is often more severe for women than for men.

To determine whether workers in a declining employment industry, occupation or region who lost their jobs were in trouble, Bendick and Devine examined the long duration unemployment in March 1980 of civilian workers age 22 to 64.[3] Of the 213 industries studied, 43 displayed declining employment, and about 90,000 workers from those industries had been unemployed more than six months; one-half of those long duration unemployed came from the automobile and textile industries. Similarly, as shown in Table 5-1, 149 of the 428 occupations studied had declining employment, and there were (coincidentally) also about 90,000 long duration unemployed from these declining occupations; one-half were operatives (especially truck drivers) and one-third laborers. Those 90,000 represented only 14 percent of the long duration unemployed at that time, suggesting that declining industries and occupations account for little of the long-term unemployment problem.

Table 5-1. *Economic Dislocation of "Mainstream" Workers, Age 22-64, for Occupations Experiencing Declining Total Employment, March 1980*

| Occupation | Average Annual Change in Employment, 1977-80 (%) | Looking for Work More than 26 Weeks | Looking for Work More than 26 Weeks as % of Total Looking for Work in Occupation |
|---|---|---|---|
| | | % | |
| Operatives | −3.8 | 43,017 | 8.9 | 7.0 |
| Laborers | −3.7 | 27,551 | 5.7 | 10.0 |
| Craftspeople and kindred workers | −3.1 | 7,140 | 1.5 | 5.4 |
| Service workers | −3.8 | 4,177 | 0.9 | 9.8 |
| Professional, technical, managerial, and sales workers | −2.9 | 4,402 | 0.9 | 12.7 |
| Clerical and kindred workers | −3.3 | 3,423 | 0.7 | 9.5 |
| 149 occupations experiencing employment decline | −3.5 | 89,710 | 18.5 | 7.6 |
| 279 occupations experiencing employment growth | 7.7 | 396,194 | 81.5 | 11.4 |
| All 428 occupations | 4.0 | 485,904 | 100.0 | 9.6 |

Source: Special tabulations of the *Current Population Survey* (March 1980), reported in Marc Bendick, Jr. and Judith R. Devine, "Workers Dislocated by Economic Change: Do They Need Federal Employment and Training Assistance?" *Appendix B, Seventh Annual Report of the National Commission for Employment Policy* (October 1981).

Bendick and Devine calculated that unemployed workers from a declining employment industry or occupation did not typically suffer *longer* duration unemployment than did workers from nondeclining industries or occupations.[4] Further, those dislocated workers had several special characteristics: they tended to have at least a high school education, to be less likely than other long-term unemployed to be minorities or women, and to have higher incomes in the year prior to their job loss. However, some of their worst adjustment problems stemmed from their relative affluence: they tended to own homes that made them less mobile and to have higher wages and fringe benefits that made them more likely to wait for a recall. For example, the total compensation of automobile and steel workers in 1980 was 50 percent greater than that of the average worker in U.S. manufacturing with similar skills, and half of that differential had been gained just over the 1970s. Finally, the dislocated workers from declining industries and occupations tended to have higher family incomes—60 percent had other earners in the family. They were also more likely in the late 1970s to collect unemployment insurance and other forms of wage replacement derived from the Trade Adjustment Assistance program or other sources.

Although a declining industry or occupation does not, in itself, appear to produce unusually long-term unemployment, a declining *region* clearly does. Bendick and Devine examined regional decline in population and employment in 44 geographic areas and found a substantial amount of long duration unemployment concentrated in particular regions. In fact, if only regions with declines in population are counted (since some growing areas have high unemployment because of an influx of job seekers),[5] there were about 180,000 long-term unemployed from declining regions in 1980. Further, they found that job losers in declining areas or labor markets were much more likely to be in distress and to suffer long duration unemployment. This is consistent with studies of plant closings: when local unemployment is high, dislocation is more likely to lead to distress.

In total, the long duration unemployed from declining industries, occupations or regions represented less than 0.5 percent of the labor force and less than 5 percent of the unemployed in March 1980. Dislocation is more likely to be associated with long duration unemployment, and hence distress, if it occurs in a declining region. Of course, distress depends on the earnings loss, not just on the duration of unemployment. Estimates suggest that in automobile and steel (where earnings are unusually high), long-term total earnings losses exceed $20,000 per displaced worker and are greatest for those with 8 to 10 years of job tenure.[6]

## Industrial, Occupational and Regional Changes in the 1980s

How will likely future developments in the industrial, occupational and regional structure of jobs affect the extent and kind of displacement in the 1980s? Two factors affecting these developments stand out in particular: international trade and technological change.

Increasing foreign trade involves an expansion of jobs in goods or services for which the United States has a comparative advantage and a job contraction in goods or services for which it has the least advantage. A nation cannot have exports without imports. But production of the exports need not involve the same numbers or kinds of jobs as the production of the imports. For example, the United States has a strong comparative advantage in agriculture and computers and has an apparent comparative disadvantage in clothing, textiles and steel. Furthermore, international capital movements can give this country a significant trade imbalance, and thus a net loss of jobs, over an extended period of time. So trade, while good for the nation overall, can cause significant adjustment problems.

The goods in which the United States has had a comparative disadvantage tend, on average, to be goods made by poorer, less educated workers.[7] That workforce also includes a much higher percentage of women than does the overall manufacturing workforce. The poverty rate among workers in the 20 industries in which imports have been increasing most prominently is two-thirds higher than the poverty rate in the 20 industries in which the United States has the greatest advantage. This often makes it easier to justify compensating workers adversely affected by international trade, since they are often the low income workers to begin with. The imported share of U.S. consumption of manufactures is likely to continue increasing in this decade, so the same pressures on jobs and wages will be at work, and those dislocated and in distress may need some help. However, the experience with the Trade Adjustment Assistance program has been that 70 percent of workers who received compensation because of trade-related job losses returned to work for the same firm within six months, illustrating how difficult it often is to identify who among laid-off workers is in long-term trouble.[8]

The second major source of job dislocation is technological change, and here the incidence of effects is less clear cut. As indicated in Chapter 2, the new techniques of production have tended to compress the distribution of skills, eliminating some of the more skilled as well as the less skilled jobs.[9] Since the equipment embodying the new production techniques is costly, technological changes often occur either where labor is unwilling or unavailable to perform certain jobs or where unusually high wages provide incentives to eliminate jobs. Of course, technological change also occurs for other reasons, such as improving management, increasing quality or producing new products or services.

New longitudinal data have revealed much over the past few years about industrial dynamics and how jobs are created and destroyed.[10] There is a constant flow of establishments being born, expanding, contracting, going out of business, and moving. In most parts of the coun-

Table 5-2. Employment Levels and Changes by Industry, 1969–90

| 25 Greatest Job Creators | Employment (1,000s) 1979 Total | Employment (1,000s) Change 1979–90 | Annual Growth Rates (%) 1969–79 | Annual Growth Rates (%) 1979–90 | Annual Growth Rates in Output per Hour* 1969–79 | Annual Growth Rates in Output per Hour* 1979–90 |
|---|---|---|---|---|---|---|
| Eating & drinking places | 4,857 | 1,979 | 5.6 | 3.2 | −1.4 | −0.1 |
| Retail trade, except eating & drinking places | 11,951 | 1,879 | 2.1 | 1.3 | 1.9 | 1.1 |
| Hospitals | 2,614 | 1,354 | 3.9 | 3.9 | 2.0 | 0.4 |
| Business services | 3,173 | 1,142 | 6.5 | 2.8 | −1.5 | −0.4 |
| Medical services, exc. hospitals | 1,373 | 939 | 7.7 | 4.9 | −0.5 | −1.0 |
| Wholesale trade | 5,501 | 866 | 2.8 | 1.3 | 1.2 | 1.5 |
| Construction industry | 4,653 | 844 | 2.6 | 1.5 | −2.2 | 0.4 |
| Nonprofit organizations | 2,072 | 566 | 1.6 | 2.2 | 2.1 | 1.3 |
| Doctors' & dentists' services | 1,345 | 552 | 5.3 | 3.2 | −0.4 | 0.8 |
| Banking | 1,498 | 484 | 4.3 | 2.6 | 0.1 | 0.1 |
| Educational services | 1,718 | 381 | 3.4 | 1.8 | −2.6 | 4.0 |
| Professional services | 1,803 | 376 | 5.6 | 1.7 | −0.4 | 0.5 |
| Insurance | 1,748 | 373 | 2.5 | 1.8 | 2.0 | 0.6 |
| Truck transportation | 1,554 | 368 | 2.5 | 2.0 | 0.8 | 0.5 |
| Real estate | 1,367 | 365 | 4.8 | 2.2 | 0.3 | 0.2 |
| Hotels & lodging places | 1,543 | 344 | 3.8 | 1.8 | 0.3 | 2.3 |
| Automobile repair | 834 | 334 | 3.9 | 3.1 | 0.0 | 0.0 |
| Credit agencies & financial brokers | 900 | 274 | 3.3 | 2.4 | −1.0 | 0.1 |
| Amusement & recreation services | 768 | 261 | 4.4 | 2.7 | 0.8 | 0.8 |
| Computers & peripheral equipment | 339 | 213 | 4.2 | 4.5 | 5.7 | 2.9 |
| Maintenance & repair construction | 1,224 | 200 | 4.4 | 1.4 | −2.1 | 0.9 |
| Plastic products | 494 | 165 | 4.4 | 2.6 | 3.1 | 0.2 |
| Communications, exc. radio & TV | 1,121 | 159 | 2.0 | 1.2 | 5.8 | 0.6 |
| State & local gov't. enterprises, nec. | 541 | 154 | 4.4 | 2.3 | −3.0 | 0.8 |
| Coal mining | 261 | 151 (75)** | 6.6 | 4.2 (2.0)** | −3.5 | 1.8 (3.0)** |

Industrial, Occupational & Regional Changes    51

Table 5-2 Continued. Employment Levels and Changes by Industry, 1969-90

| 25 Greatest Job Losers | Employment (1,000s) 1979 Total | Change 1979-90 | Annual Growth Rates (%) 1969-79 | Annual Growth Rates (%) 1979-90 | Annual Growth Rates in Output per Hour* 1969-70 | Annual Growth Rates in Output per Hour* 1979-90 |
|---|---|---|---|---|---|---|
| Structural clay products | 52 | −8 | −2.1 | −1.5 | 2.7 | 2.8 |
| Railroad equipment | 74 | −8 | 3.8 | −1.0 | 2.0 | 1.7 |
| Confectionary products | 80 | −9 | −0.8 | −1.1 | 2.5 | 2.0 |
| Complete guided missiles & space vehicles | 81 | −11 | −2.7 | −1.3 | 0.1 | 3.7 |
| Food products, nec. | 160 | −12 | 0.6 | −0.7 | 1.4 | 4.4 |
| Saw mills & planing mills | 237 | −15 | 0.3 | −0.6 (−2.0)** | 1.4 | 2.2 |
| Radio & TV receiving sets | 116 | −17 | −2.9 | −1.5 | 6.8 | 4.7 |
| Synthetic fibers | 112 | −19 | −1.6 | −1.7 | 9.0 | 3.7 |
| Cotton | 142 | −20 | −2.2 | −1.4 | 5.7 | 3.9 |
| Leather products, inc. footwear | 232 | −20 | −3.0 | −0.8 | 1.2 | 1.9 |
| Alcoholic beverages | 86 | −24 | −1.2 | −2.9 | 4.8 | 5.4 |
| Water transportation | 222 | −25 | −0.5 | −1.1 | 5.5 | 3.4 |
| Petroleum refining & related products | 210 | −26 | 1.4 | −1.2 | 1.6 | −0.5 |
| Canned & frozen foods | 316 | −27 | 0.8 | −0.8 | 2.4 | 2.4 |
| Dairy products | 189 | −30 | −3.1 | −1.6 | 6.3 | 3.4 |
| Bakery products | 238 | −34 | −1.8 | −1.4 | 2.3 | 1.6 |
| Logging | 149 | −35 | 0.8 | −2.4 | 4.3 | 2.4 |
| Food & grain feeds | 639 | −47 | 0.1 | −0.7 | 2.7 | 4.0 |
| Millwork, plywood & wood products, nec. | 393 | −49 (−100)** | 2.4 | −1.2 (−2.5)** | 3.0 | 2.6 |
| Motor vehicles | 991 | −69 | 0.8 | −0.7 | 2.9 | 2.4 |
| Meat & livestock products | 528 | −75 | −3.5 | −1.4 | 5.4 | 3.5 |
| Railroad transportation | 560 | −97 | −1.5 | −1.7 | 2.6 | 4.4 |
| Households | 1,723 | −147 | −2.9 | −0.8 | 0.2 | 0.0 |
| Dairy & poultry products, nec. | 511 | −156 (−75)** | −4.5 | −3.3 (1.6)** | 6.8 | 6.8 |
| Agricultural products, nec. | 995 | −181 | −1.1 | −1.8 | 4.6 | 4.0 |

*Output per hour for all workers in 1972 dollars.
**Revisions in BLS estimates made by industry analysts at the First National Bank of Chicago.
nec. = not elsewhere classified.
Source: Bureau of Labor Statistics, special tabulations from "low" projections.

try, half the jobs are terminated every five years; what distinguishes regions gaining employment is that jobs are created even more rapidly. Jobs tend to be created in small, young businesses in which employment is highly volatile. Because many of these small establishments are owned by large companies, the proportion of the labor force working for small businesses has been fairly steady. Contrary to some earlier reports, small businesses account for the same minority of new jobs as in the recent past. Actual relocations of firms account for only a small proportion of jobs lost or gained in an area; net new jobs are generated in an area through differential growth rates in firms.

While the future industrial structure is not precisely known, the Bureau of Labor Statistics has been relatively accurate in its employment predictions, especially for the larger categories. Table 5-2 shows BLS predictions of the 25 industries that will add the most jobs by 1990. These account for almost 15 million new jobs, about three-quarters of the projected job growth by that year. Most of the new jobs are in eating and drinking establishments, wholesale and retail trade, and services.[11] Although there is much discussion of the job potential of "high technology" industries, they do not directly employ many people (5 to 10 percent of the workforce depending on who is included) and are not expected to increase their share of employment over the decade.[12] These industries may, of course, be crucial in affecting the U.S. trade position both directly and through their impact on the productivity of other industries, but they will not directly absorb many workers. The notion that vast portions of the workforce will have to be or can be retooled and sent to those industries is unfounded.

This point can be illustrated with the data in Table 5-3, which displays BLS occupational projections ranked two ways. The left-hand columns are the highest growth *rate* occupations; many deal with computers and are the high technology areas that attract great attention. But from the point of view of the economy and the average worker, the important occupations are those with the highest growth in *numbers* of jobs. Shown in the right-hand columns, that list is quite different. It accounts for over one-third of the new jobs, versus one-tenth for the other list. With the exception of nurses, teachers and accountants, these jobs require relatively modest amounts of post-high school training. Recent discussions about massive dislocations and the need for a complete restructuring of the workforce do not stand up to such analyses. Although some restructuring must occur, the pace is likely to be manageable.

Finally, there is the question of the regional composition of employment. Dislocation is most serious when it is concentrated geographically, but it is very difficult to predict where employment will decline. The Great Lakes region is in trouble, but this may be heavily influenced by the current recession in consumer durables brought on by tight monetary policy over several years. Employment in the automobile industry was at an historic high in 1978 before the recession started and,

Table 5-3. Occupations Projected to Have Highest Growth by 1990, Rate Versus Number of Employees

| 20 Highest Growth Rate Occupations | Percent Growth in Employment, 1978-90 | Growth in Employment (in 1,000s), 1978-90 | 20 Highest Growth (in Numbers) Occupations | Growth in Employment (in 1,000s), 1978-90 |
|---|---|---|---|---|
| Data processing machine mechanics | 147.6 | 93 | Janitors & sextons | 671.2 |
| Paralegal personnel | 132.4 | 38 | Nurses aides & orderlies | 594.0 |
| Computer systems analysts | 107.8 | 199 | Sales clerks | 590.7 |
| Computer operators | 87.9 | 148 | Cashiers | 545.5 |
| Office machine & cash register servicers | 80.8 | 40 | Waiters/waitresses | 531.9 |
| Computer programmers | 73.6 | 150 | General clerks, office | 529.8 |
| Aero-astronautic engineers | 70.4 | 41 | Professional nurses | 515.8 |
| Food preparation & service workers, fast food restaurants | 68.8 | 492 | Food preparation & service workers, fast food restaurants | 491.9 |
| Employment interviewers | 66.6 | 35 | Secretaries | 487.8 |
| Tax preparers | 64.5 | 18 | Truck drivers | 437.6 |
| Correction officials & jailers | 60.3 | 57 | Kitchen helpers | 300.6 |
| Architects | 60.2 | 40 | Elementary school teachers | 272.8 |
| Dental hygienists | 57.9 | 31 | Typists | 262.1 |
| Physical therapists | 57.6 | 18 | Accountants & auditors | 254.2 |
| Dental assistants | 57.5 | 70 | Helpers, trades | 232.5 |
| Peripheral EDP equipment operators | 57.3 | 26 | Blue-collar worker supervisors | 221.1 |
| Child-care attendants | 56.3 | 20 | Bookkeepers, hand | 219.7 |
| Veterinarians | 56.1 | 17 | Licensed practical nurses | 215.6 |
| Travel agents & accommodations appraisers | 55.6 | 25 | Guards & doorkeepers | 209.9 |
| Nurses aides & orderlies | 54.6 | 594 | Automotive mechanics | 205.3 |
| Total | | 2,152 | Total | 7,790 |

Source: Max L. Carey, "Occupational Employment Growth Through 1990," *Monthly Labor Review* (August 1981), p. 48.

while it may never return to those levels, it could make a substantial comeback.

When decline does occur, the transformation of a region's economy can take decades, as it did in New England following the emigration of textiles. However, migration flows tend to be self-limiting. Discussions of the continued migration of jobs to the West and the Sunbelt, for instance, often ignore the fact that much of the regional equalization that will cause these flows to abate has already occurred. Figure 5-1 shows that per capita personal income differences among regions have substantially disappeared over the past half century. The creation of a national economy with a unified transportation system has been an enormous source of regional mobility, leading to regional equality. Major regional disparities in growth rates might thus be coming to an end.

There is one important caveat to this optimistic view of regional trends. Much of the improvement in average incomes in the South has

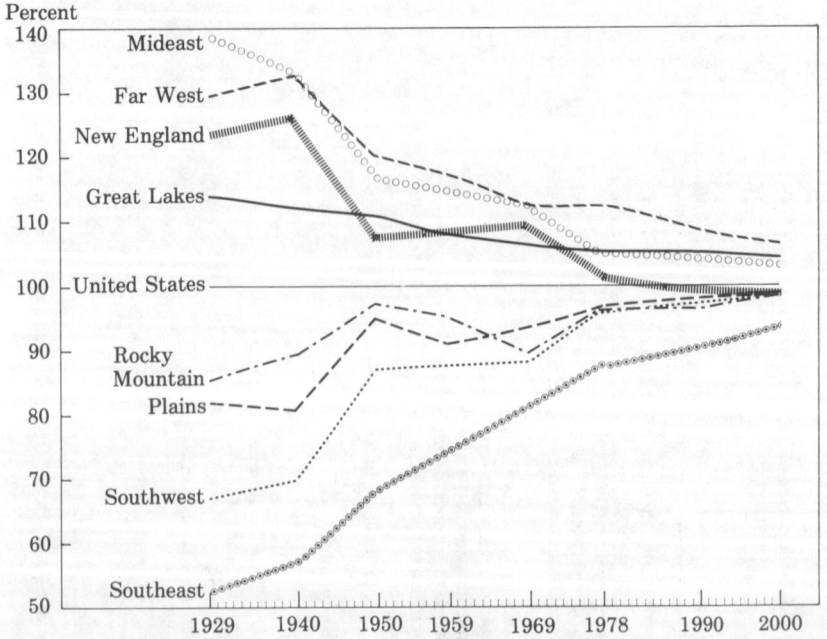

Figure 5-1. *Per Capita Personal Income as a Percent of the U.S. Average, Selected Years, 1929–2000, Bureau of Economic Analysis Regions*

Source: U.S. Department of Commerce.

come from growing cities being grafted onto the region. The extreme rural poverty and labor market distress of the Mississippi Valley persist for those who have not been able or willing to escape.[13] The same tendency toward a dual economy exists in northern cities, which continue to suburbanize across old metropolitan boundaries, leaving pockets of poverty in the central cities. There is no reason to expect a reversal of these trends. Thus, the principal "regional" differences may no longer exist between North and South, East and West, but between the prosperous cities/suburbs and the poor central cities/rural areas. Minorities at the low end of the distribution of skills are caught in these depressed "regions" where labor market distress is endemic.

## Conclusion

Trade, technological change and other aspects of a dynamic economy mean changes in employment. But the evidence suggests that the overall changes in the economy will probably be gradual and that the dislocations are likely to be highly concentrated. Dislocated workers are more often in distress in declining employment labor markets or regions than in declining employment occupations or industries. Thus, policies to deal with labor market distress among dislocated workers should focus on places and people rather than on occupations and industries. Changes and dislocations will be occurring; the challenge is both to promote productive change and to anticipate and alleviate the distress.

## Notes

1 Two helpful discussions of the issue are Sar A. Levitan and Clifford M. Johnson, *Second Thoughts on Work* (Kalamazoo, Mich.: W.E. Upjohn Institute for Employment Research, 1982), p. 241, and Richard K. Vedder, "Robotics and the Economy," A Staff Study of the Subcommittee on Monetary and Fiscal Policy of the Joint Economic Committee of the Congress of the United States (March 26, 1982), p. 34.

2 National Commission for Employment Policy, *CETA Training Programs: Do They Work for Adults* (July 1982), p. A-23.

3 Marc Bendick, Jr. and Judith R. Devine, "Workers Dislocated by Economic Change: Do They Need Federal Employment and Training Assistance?" *Appendix B, Seventh Annual Report of the National Commission for Employment Policy* (October 1981). More recent estimates by Steve Sheingold of the numbers of dislocated workers can be found in the Congressional Budget Office, *Dislocated Workers: Issues and Federal Options* (July 1982). These are not reported here because they are probably too influenced by the recent disastrous business cycle activity to be a good index of structural dislocation.

4 However, their study did not look at completed periods, so the findings are suggestive at best.

5 Stephen T. Marston, *Two Views of the Geographic Distribution of Unemployment* (National Commission for Employment Policy, 1980), mimeo.

6 For a useful review, see Louis Jacobson and Janet Thompson, "Earnings Loss Due to Displacement," Working Paper 385 (Public Research Institute, Center for Naval Analyses, August 1979), p. 28.

7 Office of Foreign Research, Bureau of International Labor Affairs, "The Impact of Changes in Manufacturing Trade on Sectoral Employment Patterns—Progress Report," in National Commission for Manpower Policy, *Trade and Employment*, Special Report No. 30 (November 1978), pp. 259–312.

8 Walter Corson, "Survey of Trade Adjustment Assistance Recipients," Final Report (Washington: Department of Labor, Bureau of International Labor Affairs, September 1979).

9 For a recent discussion, see the special issue of *Scientific American* on "The Mechanization of Work," Vol. 247, No. 3 (September 1982), p. 218.

10 For a review, see Richard Greene, "Tracking Job Growth in Private Industry," *Monthly Labor Review* (September 1982), pp. 3–9.

11 Expert industry analysts at First National Bank of Chicago examined BLS projections and found little to quarrel with. Their comments are noted on Table 5-2.

12 These high technology industries usually include drugs and medicines; office, computing and accounting equipment; electrical and electronic equipment; aircraft and missiles; and instruments and related products. Some breakdowns include the broader industry groups of which these are a part.

13 Stephen F. Geninger and Timothy M. Smeeding, "Rural Poverty, Human Resources, and Welfare Policy" (USDA, Farmer's Home Administration, 1980), p. 74.

*Chapter 6*

# Distressed Older Workers

As the life cycle of work draws to a close, workers are most likely to be in distress when health or other impediments cause them to have insufficient earnings or to be out of the labor force without enough income to retire. Some of those with inadequate earnings were also in distress in earlier periods. For many older workers who have low earnings, retirement ends their agony; for others, it simply removes any remaining hope of improvement and offers the prospect of continued insecurity and poverty. This report does not discuss retirement policy for the poor or the redistributive aspects of the Social Security system. Rather, it focuses on one important dimension of distress for this group: poor health and premature retirement. Relatively little is known about this subject,[1] although it will absorb increasing attention as the baby-boom generation approaches retirement early next century.

Each year for the next few decades, about 2 million persons will reach age 65, about 15 percent more than the annual flow during the 1970s.[2] The over-65 group will be about 12 percent of the population early in this period, with that share rising to 18 percent by 2030. That increase may seem large, but it should be kept in perspective: if real GNP grows at only 1.4 percent per year, GNP will double by 2030; the real amount of Social Security and Medicare received by each retired person over age 65 could remain the same; and the share of GNP (5 percent now) used for that purpose could still decline by one-fourth. The growth in the retired population will draw attention to them, generate interest in making it easier for them to continue to work, and spur efforts to prepare for the retirement of the baby-boom generation.

The attempts to reform the Social Security system could have a particularly adverse effect on distressed older workers. As Figures 6-1 and 6-2 dramatically illustrate, Social Security rules strongly influence the age of retirement and the reported amount of post-retirement earnings for an overwhelming proportion of the elderly population. But some workers who have to retire have few other sources of income, and others are dependent on retirement income that is not available until age 65 or later. Hence, increasing the earliest age of retirement under Social Security will leave some of these early retirees in distress for longer periods. Targeted programs may be required to deal with their specialized problems. Distress is no more an average phenomenon for older workers than for the other groups discussed here.

One recent study analyzes the male retirees in a national sample who had some retirement income or disability payments starting within a year of their retirement.[3] During such "covered retirement," the level of benefits may have replaced only a small proportion of normal earnings. Over one-third of the retirees were not covered at all during at least their first year of retirement, and the chance of coverage varied substantially depending on the worker's normal earnings, wealth and health. Of workers whose normal preretirement income in 1966 dollars was less than $4,200 per year, only 36 percent had any coverage at retirement, compared to 53 percent for those with incomes between $4,200 and $6,800, and 72 percent for those with incomes greater than $6,800. People do not always retire because they can afford to: Diamond and Hausman calculated that bad health is as likely to cause early retirement as is eligibility for a $10,000 per year pension.

As a cohort approaches its fifties, there is a continued winnowing or inequality in the labor market, with distress being associated more and more with lack of employment. Table 6-1 shows that the proportion of the unemployed in each age-sex group who have been unem-

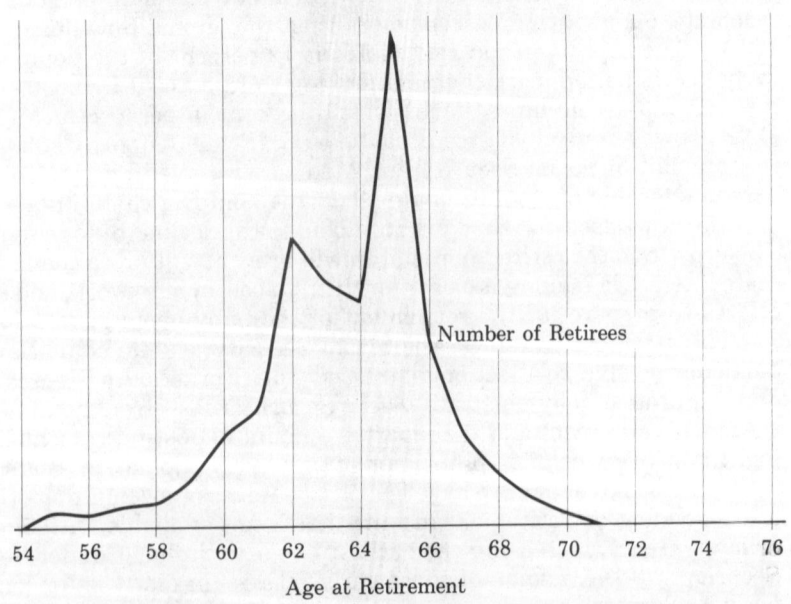

Figure 6-1. *Distribution of Retirement Ages, Retirement History Survey,\* 1969-79*

\*This national sample was restricted to able-bodied men age 58-63 in 1969 (sample size, 3,535). Those who had retired by the end of the survey were included.

Source: Gary Burtless and Robert A. Moffitt, "The Effect of Social Security on Labor Supply of the Aged: The Joint Choice of Retirement Date and Post-Retirement Hours of Work" (Washington: Brookings Institution, October 12, 1982), mineo. Reproduced with permission.

ployed for at least six months is higher for older groups. Health problems clearly play a major role here. Diamond and Hausman found that bad health increased the typical period of unemployment of fired workers by 48 percent for otherwise similar older men[4]; they also found that older men whose normal income was $5,000 (in 1966 dollars) less than the average tended to be unemployed 31 percent more of the time. Chirikos and Nestel, using detailed data on health-related work impairments, found *wages* no lower on average for impaired older workers,[5] and also that impairment caused older workers to drop out of the labor market rather than to shift to lower wage occupations. Unfortunately, the econometric techniques used by Chirikos and Nestel failed to adjust for the fact that those who were employed despite impairments may have had other exceptional characteristics. Nonetheless, their results are consistent with the idea that wages are less flexible among older cohorts, and hence labor market difficulties are more likely to lead to nonemployment.

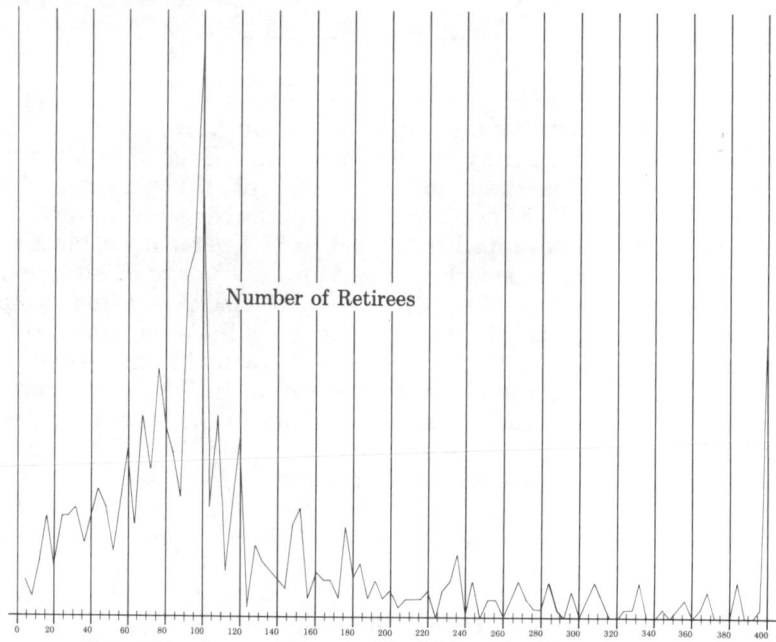

Figure 6-2. *Distribution of Retiree Earnings Around the Exempt Amount, Retirement History Survey,\* 1969-79*

Retiree Earnings as Percent of Social Security Exempt Amount

\*See note to Figure 6-1.
Source: Burtless and Moffitt, "The Effect of Social Security." Reproduced with permission.

Table 6-1. Annual Average Percent of Unemployed in a Group Who Reported Continuous Unemployment of at Least Six Months, by Age and Sex, 1968 and 1978
(Numbers in 1000s in Parentheses)

| Age Group | Male | | Female | |
|---|---|---|---|---|
| | 1968 | 1978 | 1968 | 1978 |
| Age 16-19 | 2.6 (10.9) | 4.9 (39.2) | 2.7 (10.9) | 4.6 (34.8) |
| Age 20-24 | 4.2 (10.9) | 9.6 (70.3) | 3.8 (10.9) | 7.0 (48.7) |
| Age 25-44 | 7.1 (26.8) | 14.7 (141.0) | 4.3 (18.9) | 9.7 (106.0) |
| Age 45-64 | 12.0 (35.7) | 22.1 (105.0) | 7.6 (17.9) | 14.1 (58.9) |
| Age 65+ | 17.9 (10.9) | 27.4 (22.1) | 7.5 (2.0) | 16.2 (7.0) |

Source: Author's calculations from data reported in U.S. Department of Labor, Health and Human Services, *Statistical Appendix, Employment and Training Report of the President* (1980), pp. 250, 268.

## The Decrease in Labor Force Participation of Older Males

Why is long duration nonemployment more prevalent among older workers and more typically a signal of distress? Even more important, why has the labor force participation of older males recently been declining so much? From 1970 to 1979, the labor force participation rate of males age 45 to 54 dropped from 88.0 to 85.5 percent for blacks and from 95 to 92 percent for whites, while for males age 55-64 the drop was much greater (from 79 to 67 percent for blacks and from 83 to 74 percent for whites). This is another example of the bifurcation problem discussed in Chapter 4. While differences in earnings among employed workers may be narrowing, the important inequality seems to be between those who are and those who are not in the labor force. Some possible explanations for the decline in the older worker participation in the labor market are discussed below.

(1) *Mandatory retirement programs.* This is a small source of distress. Of retired men age 65 to 69 in the National Longitudinal Survey, only 5 percent of whites and 8 percent of blacks gave this in explanation for their retirement.[6] Poor health was the cause of retirement cited by 47 percent of blacks and 38 percent of whites, while 57 percent of whites and 45 percent of blacks described their retirement as voluntary. Even when subject to mandatory retirement, only 14 percent of

whites and 26 percent of blacks reported that as the actual reason for retirement.

(2) **Low potential earnings.** Older workers with little education find a substantially lower payoff to working. Older men with less than four years of education who were working in 1976 had family incomes only $1,800 higher than those who were not working. For those with high school diplomas, the differential was $5,000.[7] The effect of education is so strong that the labor force participation rates of older black and white males with similar levels of school attainment are almost equal. Thus, the low earning members of a cohort tend to become the nonemployed members when the cohort reaches its fifties.

(3) **Special characteristics of the labor market for older workers.** Just as younger workers are expected to have a high incidence of short duration unemployment, there are reasons to expect older workers to have a high incidence of long duration unemployment or nonemployment, even apart from health and similar problems. First, older workers are likely to have become particularly valuable to the firm where they were working and are unlikely to find another employer who would value them as highly. Second, older workers may have been getting "rents" in their old jobs because they were union members or senior employees, or for other reasons, and such wage advantages are hard to find again. Third, on the employer's side, there may be larger fixed costs in employing an older worker, especially if the firm has a defined benefit retirement plan. Finally, there is age discrimination: older workers may be automatically fired or not hired, or there may be stereotypes about absenteeism, poor health or other productivity-related characteristics among the elderly. The age discrimination issue is extremely complex, and proposed solutions can create new problems. For example, if it is made costly to fire less productive *individuals*, then employers are more likely to adopt age discrimination in hiring or other measures against less productive *groups*.

(4) **Increasing Social Security Disability payments.** Disability payments (at least 50 percent from Social Security) accounted for 29 percent of the family income of white men age 45 to 59 who were out of the labor force in 1965 (48 percent for similar black men). Higher disability payment levels and easier availability could cause more of those with marginal health to choose not to be in the labor force. It is true that the Social Security Disability and Insurance (SSDI) program expanded dramatically during the first half of the 1970s and may have absorbed many who would otherwise have been characterized as distressed workers in poor health but not incapacitated.[8] However, the growth in this program moderated substantially during the second half of the 1970s, perhaps because the economy improved and the stock of

eligible people was largely enrolled by the middle of the decade. Recently, there has been a concerted effort to reduce the rolls, and since 1979, 400,000 fewer persons are in the program. In the first two years of the Reagan Administration (1981–82), over 100,000 persons were removed from the rolls in a controversial eligibility crackdown.

Although the disability program provides some inducements for dropping out of the labor force, early studies appear to have vastly exaggerated its role in explaining declining labor force participation of older males. Haveman, Wolfe and Warlick estimated that a 10 percent increase in expected benefits reduces labor supply by .005 percent, with the greatest responsiveness for those with the lowest labor market earnings capacity. They concluded that few categories of recipients could be removed from the rolls (with the exceptions of alcoholics and those who would be in the upper income groups without SSDI) without causing at least a one-third reduction of income and substantial hardship. The SSDI program has clearly played an important role in allowing those who would have been in labor market distress for health reasons (broadly defined) to get out of the labor market. The cutbacks in that program will put many of them back in the market, with effects on distress that will depend on how the rolls are cut; those least in economic need may be more likely to have gotten their benefits through appeals and may be the most difficult to dislodge through bureaucratic procedures.

## Widowhood

Because of the large mortality differential between men and women, widows, especially those with little labor market experience, are often in distress. This problem may decrease, however, as potential widows come increasingly from newer cohorts of women who have had more labor market experience. But for older women, as for others, a change in family composition is more likely to alter poverty status than is a change in earnings, and widowhood is the prime cause of family change for this group. Further, widowhood is much more likely in poor and black families, another reminder that poor labor market performance is strongly associated with loss of health and early death. Calculations from the National Longitudinal Survey indicate that the poverty rate among older women age 45 to 59 was 3 percent for whites and 16 percent for blacks.[9] For those women who became widowed over the sample period, the poverty rate prior to their husband's death was 19 percent for whites and 47 percent for blacks; after being widowed, the poverty rate rose to 29 percent for whites and 67 percent for blacks. The earnings of these women accounted for 18 percent of family income prior to widowhood and 30 percent afterward. In short, the loss of the husband's earnings, even considering any survivor's benefits, caused a substantial number of women suddenly to become earnings poor.

## Conclusion

For older workers, as for the other groups discussed here, distress is concentrated among a relatively small part of the cohort, many of whom were earnings poor at earlier ages. But at this stage, the problem is more likely to take the form of long duration nonemployment and health-induced retirement, rather than unemployment or low wages. The SSDI program has become, perhaps accidentally, an income support program for many older workers because they are much more likely to have health problems. The increased flow of older workers into the labor market caused by cutbacks in the SSDI program suggests that this group of distressed workers will be growing over the 1980s.

## Notes

1 Research was initiated on this question while the author was Director of the National Commission for Employment Policy. That research has moved forward in cooperation with the Labor Department and should be available in 1983.

2 A useful discussion of the issues raised here can be found in Bruce Vavrichek, *Work and Retirement: Options for Continued Employment of Older Workers* (Congressional Budget Office, July 1982).

3 The following calculations are based on tabulations for a national sample provided in Peter Diamond and Jerry Hausman, "Retirement and Unemployment Behavior of Older Men" (Washington: Brookings Institution, October 1982), mimeo.

4 Ibid., p. 40. The authors have exercised special care to account for some potentially important estimation problems. However, they look at retirement as a discrete choice. Burtless and Moffitt examine the retirement and post-retirement hours of work decision jointly, which appears more useful. Unfortunately, the complexities of their model have limited the number of variables that could be included in their currently available analysis. See Gary Burtless and Robert A. Moffitt, "The Effect of Social Security on Labor Supply of the Aged: The Joint Choice of Retirement Data and Post-Retirement Hours of Work" (Washington: Brookings Institution, October 12, 1982), mimeo.

5 Thomas N. Chirikos and Gilbert Nestel, "Impairment and Labor Market Outcomes: A Cross Sectional and Longitudinal Analysis," in Herbert S. Parnes, ed., *Work and Retirement, A Longitudinal Study of Men* (Cambridge, Mass.: MIT Press, 1981), pp. 93-131. As with other studies that use this sample, there may be serious problems of attrition bias.

6 Herbert S. Parnes and Gilbert Nestel, "The Retirement Experience," in Parnes, *Work and Retirement*, pp. 155-197.

7 Donald O. Parsons, "Black-White Differences in Labor Force Participation of Older Males," in Parnes, *Work and Retirement*, pp. 132-154.

8 The following is taken from a paper by Robert Haveman, Barbara Wolfe and Jennifer L. Warlick, "Disability Transfers, Early Retirement, and Retrenchment: Do Disability Benefit Levels Cause Less Work? Does Retrenchment Cause Hardships?" (Washington:

Brookings Institution, October 1982), mimeo. The problem with all of this research is that it is very difficult to estimate the labor market earnings the SSDI recipients would have received.

9 Frank L. Mot and R. Jean Haurin, "The Impact of Health Problems and Mortality on Family Well-Being," in Parnes, *Work and Retirement,* pp. 222–223.

Chapter 7
# Final Note

For the 11 million or so Americans who were earnings poor at the beginning of this decade, the message of this report has been dismally clear: the extent and severity of their labor market distress will probably increase over the 1980s, as favorable supply-side trends are likely to be offset by unfavorable demand conditions. Even if economic recovery is strong enough to reduce overall unemployment significantly, serious structural problems in the labor market will leave concentrated groups in distress.

The starting point for the decade was a relatively healthy labor market, which is a fundamental requirement for dealing with structural labor market problems. In such circumstances, distress is concentrated in identifiable groups. In the weak labor market of the early 1980s, about the best that can be hoped for is that the incomes of these groups can be maintained with the help of public programs. This period of weak demand can also be used for projects that train distressed workers for better jobs later or that build and repair needed public and private capital; certainly there are many such tasks that might be undertaken.

While the focus of this report has not been on programs and policies, some that can be effective tools will be mentioned here. Many of these tend to be costly because they must try to offset long-standing and serious problems, but they still may be worth the expense. And because the problems of the different groups in distress are so different, the solutions must be tailored to each group.

For young people having difficulty as they enter the labor force, policies to consider include extending compensatory education to secondary schools, developing alternative schools for high school dropouts, and offering intensive residential training such as the Job Corps. Those entering school in the 1980s will need to obtain the basic skills required in an automated service society—literacy and numeracy.

For adults whose labor market distress is persistent, part of the answer may be in income maintenance programs that encourage them to work and in wage subsidies that encourage others to hire them. However, both approaches have some difficulties. Wage subsidies that affect labor demand can stigmatize the eligible workers. The income maintenance experiments of the 1970s demonstrated that the poor as well as the rich respond to incentives, a fact that is a two-edged sword. Allowing welfare recipients to work without losing all their benefits (e.g., with a negative income tax) induces them to work more, thereby reducing welfare payments; but it also induces less work among low earners in the labor market who qualify for both welfare and higher tax rates under such schemes. Increased costs among the more numerous working poor exceed the savings among the traditional welfare recipients. If the working poor are to be subsidized, it will have to be because society decides that they "deserve" (and that their children will benefit from) being removed from poverty, not because it will save welfare costs in the short run. Many disadvantaged adults can also be assisted with well-designed employment and training programs.

For dislocated adult workers with a history of adequate earnings, the problem is to determine who is in distress as a result of displacement and to design programs to help them without inhibiting the adjustment of others. For example, the long duration unemployed who are not candidates for retirement often require special help. Yet, assistance that is conditional on long-term unemployment may discourage some workers from taking lesser opportunities after a shorter period of unemployment. Professional employment counselors might be able to identify those with the most serious problems, although this is beyond the typical capacity of our current employment and training institutions.

The distress of older workers occurs at a stage in life when it is often too late to provide effective relief. The deteriorating health of these workers reinforces their problems. Identifying and dealing with the correctable problems at an earlier stage appears to be the solution. This requires a renewed commitment to education, nutrition and other human resource development policies. Once the older worker's health fails, the problem is to supply aid in the most humane and efficient way. Yet, programs that help may also create adverse incentives for the older worker whose condition is borderline. Recognition of these unavoidable conflicts is the first step to a mature human resource system.

The dimensions of labor market distress are far better known now than they were a few years ago. A concentrated group of at least 11 million distressed workers existed even before the recession of the early 1980s and is likely to remain even if economic recovery is strong. These people work or would work if they could, yet they are in distress. There are many subgroups, and each requires different kinds of help and incentives. The people in distress at one age are often the same who were or will be in distress at other ages. Thus, the earlier in life the distress-prone individuals are identified, the more cost-effective and humane assistance is likely to be.

# National Planning Association

NPA is an independent, private, nonprofit, nonpolitical organization that carries on research and policy formulation in the public interest. NPA was founded during the Great Depression of the 1930s when conflicts among the major economic groups—business, labor, agriculture—threatened to paralyze national decisionmaking on the critical issues confronting American society. It was dedicated to the task of getting these diverse groups to work together to narrow areas of controversy and broaden areas of agreement and to provide on specific problems concrete programs for action planned in the best traditions of a functioning democracy. Such democratic planning, NPA believes, involves the development of effective governmental and private policies and programs not only by official agencies but also through the independent initiative and cooperation of the main private-sector groups concerned. And to preserve and strengthen American political and economic democracy, the necessary government actions have to be consistent with, and stimulate the support of, a dynamic private sector.

NPA brings together influential and knowledgeable leaders from business, labor, agriculture, and the applied and academic professions to serve on policy committees. These committees identify emerging problems confronting the nation at home and abroad and seek to develop and agree upon policies and programs for coping with them. The research and writing for these committees are provided by NPA's professional staff and, as required, by outside experts.

In addition, NPA's professional staff undertakes research designed to provide data and ideas for policymakers and planners in government and the private sector. These activities include the preparation on a regular basis of economic and demographic projections for the national economy, regions, states, metropolitan areas, and counties; research on national goals and priorities, productivity and economic growth, welfare and dependency problems, employment and manpower needs, and energy and environmental questions; analyses and forecasts of changing international realities and their implications for U.S. policies; and analyses of important new economic, social and political realities confronting American society. In developing its staff capabilities, NPA has increasingly emphasized two related qualifications. First is the development of the interdisciplinary knowledge required to understand the complex nature of many real-life problems. Second is the ability to bridge the gap between theoretical or highly technical research and the practical needs of policymakers and planners in government and the private sector.

All NPA reports have been authorized for publication in accordance with procedures laid down by the Board of Trustees. Such action does not imply agreement by NPA board or committee members with all that is contained therein unless such endorsement is specifically stated.

# NPA Officers and Board of Trustees

WALTER STERLING SURREY
*Chairman;* Senior Partner, Surrey and Morse

MURRAY H. FINLEY
*Chairman, Executive Committee;* President, Amalgamated Clothing & Textile Workers' Union

ALEXANDER C. TOMLINSON
*President;* NPA

DALE M. HOOVER
*Vice Chairman;* Chairman, Department of Economics and Business, North Carolina State University

JOSEPH D. KEENAN
*Vice Chairman;* Washington, D.C.

JOHN MILLER
*Vice Chairman;* Alexandria, Virginia

STEPHEN C. EYRE
*Treasurer;* Citicorp Professor of Finance, Pace University

WILLIAM W. WINPISINGER
*Secretary;* President, International Association of Machinists & Aerospace Workers

SPERRY LEA
*Vice President;* NPA

PETER G. MORICI
*Vice President;* NPA

LARRY E. RUFF
*Vice President;* NPA

WAYNE E. SWEGLE
*Vice President;* NPA

NESTOR E. TERLECKYJ
*Vice President;* NPA

W.B. BEHNKE
Vice Chairman, Commonwealth Edison

PHILIP BRIGGS
Executive Vice President, Metropolitan Life Insurance Company

KENNETH J. BROWN
President, Graphic Communications International Union

ROBERT K. BUCK
Waukee, Iowa

EDWARD J. CARLOUGH
General President, Sheet Metal Workers' International Association

SOL C. CHAIKIN
President, International Ladies' Garment Workers' Union

J.G. CLARKE
Director and Senior Vice President, Exxon Corporation

JACOB CLAYMAN
President, National Council of Senior Citizens, Inc.

G.A. COSTANZO
New York, New York

EDWARD L. CUSHMAN
Clarence Hilberry University Professor, Wayne State University

JOHN DIEBOLD
Chairman, The Diebold Group, Inc.

THOMAS W. diZEREGA
Upperville, Virginia

WILLIAM D. EBERLE
Chairman, EBCO Incorporated

DOUGLAS A. FRASER
President, International Union, United Automobile, Aerospace & Agricultural Implement Workers of America-UAW

ROBERT M. FREDERICK
Legislative Director, National Grange

ROBERT R. FREDERICK
President, RCA Corporation

RALPH W. GOLBY
Vice President, Investor Relations, Schering-Plough Corporation

JEROME S. GORE
Chairman and Chief Executive Officer, Hartmarx Corporation

TERRY HERNDON
Washington, D.C.

G. GRIFFITH JOHNSON, JR.
Sherwood Forest, Md.

MARY GARDINER JONES
President, Consumer Interest Research Institute

PETER T. JONES
Senior Vice President and General Counsel, Levi Strauss & Company

EDWARD G. JORDAN
President, The American College

LANE KIRKLAND
President, AFL-CIO

JUANITA KREPS
Durham, North Carolina

## NPA Officers & Board

PETER F. KROGH
Dean, Edmund A. Walsh School of Foreign Service, Georgetown University

JOHN H. LYONS
General President, International Association of Bridge, Structural and Ornamental Iron Workers

LLOYD McBRIDE
International President, United Steelworkers of America, AFL-CIO, CLC

WILLIAM J. McDONOUGH
Executive Vice President and Chief Financial Officer, The First National Bank of Chicago

JOHN W. MACY, JR.
McLean, Virginia

CHARLES MARSHALL
Chairman and Chief Executive Office, American Bell

FRANK D. MARTINO
President, Chemical Workers Union International

WILLIAM R. MILLER
President, Pharmaceutical and Nutritional Group, Bristol-Myers Company

HARRY E. MORGAN, JR.
Senior Vice President, Weyerhauser Company

RODNEY W. NICHOLS
Executive Vice President, The Rockefeller University

WILLIAM S. OGDEN
Chairman of the Interim Board of Directors, Institute of International Finance

DEAN P. PHYPERS
Senior Vice President, IBM Corporation

GEORGE J. POULIN
General Vice President, International Association of Machinists & Aerospace Workers

S. FRANK RAFTERY
General President, International Brotherhood of Painters & Allied Trades

RALPH RAIKES
Ashland, Nebraska

JOHN S. REED
Vice Chairman, Citibank, N.A.

THOMAS A. REED
Senior Corporate Vice President, Honeywell, Inc.

CARL E. REICHARDT
President, Wells Fargo Bank

WILLIAM D. ROGERS
Partner, Arnold & Porter

STANLEY H. RUTTENBERG
President, Ruttenberg, Friedman, Kilgallon, Gutchess & Associates, Inc.

HOWARD D. SAMUEL
President, Industrial Union Department, AFL-CIO

NATHANIEL SAMUELS
Advisory Director, Lehman Brothers Kuhn Loeb, Inc.

RICHARD J. SCHMEELK
Managing Director and Member of the Executive Committee, Salomon Brothers Inc.

REX A. SEBASTIAN
Senior Vice President, Operations, Dresser Industries, Inc.

LAUREN K. SOTH
Journalist, West Des Moines, Iowa

ELMER B. STAATS
Washington, D.C.

JOHN STENCEL
President, Rocky Mountain Farmers Union

MILAN STONE
URW International President, United Rubber, Cork, Linoleum and Plastic Workers of America, AFL-CIO, CLC

J.C. TURNER
General President, International Union of Operating Engineers, AFL-CIO

THOMAS N. URBAN
President and Chief Executive Officer, Pioneer Hi-Bred International

JAMES D. WATSON
Director, Cold Spring Harbor Laboratory

GLENN E. WATTS
President, Communications Workers of America, AFL-CIO

WILLIAM L. WEARLY
Chairman, Executive Committee, Ingersoll-Rand Company

GEORGE L-P WEAVER
Consultant, ORT Technical Assistance

LLOYD B. WESCOTT
Hunterdon Hills Holsteins, Inc.

RICHARD WARREN WHEELER
Bronxville, New York

LYNN R. WILLIAMS
International Secretary, United Steelworkers of America, AFL-CIO, CLC

ROBERT A. WILSON
Vice President, Public Affairs, Pfizer, Inc.

CHARLES G. WOOTTON
Senior Director, Public Affairs, Gulf Oil Corporation

WILLIAM H. WYNN
International President, United Food & Commercial Workers International Union, AFL-CIO, CLC

RALPH S. YOHE
Editor, *Wisconsin Agriculturist*

## HONORARY TRUSTEES

SOLOMON BARKIN
Department of Economics, University of Massachusetts

LUTHER H. GULICK
Chairman of the Board, Institute of Public Administration

JAMES G. PATTON
Menlo Park, California

**LIBRARY OF DAVIDSON COLLEGE**

Books on regular loan may be checked out for **two weeks.** Books must be presented at the Circulation Desk in order to be renewed.

charged after date d